Steve Allen's Songs

Steve Allen's Songs

100 LYRICS WITH COMMENTARY

by Steve Allen

with a foreword by
Gene Lees

McFarland & Company, Inc., Publishers
Jefferson, North Carolina, and London

Cover and frontispiece photographs of Steve Allen provided by Steve Allen
Back cover: "Artist's Hands," copyright Rena Small 1997

Library of Congress Cataloguing-in-Publication Data

Allen, Steve, 1921–
Steve Allen's songs : 100 lyrics with commentary /
by Steve Allen ; with a foreword by Gene Lees.
p. cm.
Includes index.
ISBN 0-7864-0736-0
(illustrated case binding : 55# alkaline paper) ∞
1. Songs, English — United States — Texts.
2. Popular music — United States — Texts.
I. Title.
ML54.6.A43S84 1999 782.42164'0268 — dc21
99-42567 CIP

British Library Cataloguing-in-Publication data are available

Manufactured in the United States of America

McFarland & Company, Inc., Publishers
Box 611, Jefferson, North Carolina 28640
www.mcfarlandpub.com

To Gene Lees,
a fine lyricist and important cultural historian,
for keeping alive the flame that must eternally
burn before the altar of excellence

Song Credits

Words and music of all songs by Steve Allen, Copyright © Meadowlane Music Inc. ASCAP (all rights reserved, international copyright secured — used by permission), with the following exceptions:

"Gravy Waltz," lyric by Steve Allen, music by Ray Brown; Copyright © 1963, renewed 1991 Ray Brown Music (BMI). All rights reserved, international copyright secured — used by permission.

"I Think We've Kinda Lost Our Way," lyric by Steve Allen, music by Louis Bellson and Jack Hayes; 1982 copyright © 1982 Jockey Music Inc. / Chroma Music Company, Inc. ASCAP. All rights reserved, international copyright secured — used by permission.

"Picnic" from the motion picture *Picnic*, lyric by Steve Allen, music by George Duning; copyright © 1956, renewed 1984 Columbia Pictures Music c/o Shapiro, Bernstein & Co. Film Division. All rights reserved, international copyright secured — used by permission.

"Solitaire," lyric by Steve Allen, music by Erroll Garner; copyright © 1960, renewed 1988 Octave Music ASCAP. All rights reserved, international copyright secured — used by permission.

"The South Rampart Street Parade," lyric by Steve Allen, music by Ray Bauduc and Bob Haggart; copyright © 1952, renewed 1980 EMI Feist Catalog Inc. All rights reserved, international copyright secured — used by permission of Warner Bros. Publications U.S. Inc., Miami, FL 33014.

Theme from *Bell, Book and Candle*, lyric by Steve Allen, music by George Duning; copyright © 1958, renewed 1986 Columbia Pictures Music c/o Shapiro, Bernstein & Co. Film Division. All rights reserved, international copyright secured — used by permission.

"Cold," lyric by Steve Allen, music by Larry Cansler; copyright 1970 Warner-Tamberlane Publishing Corp. and Meadowlane Music Inc. ASCAP. All rights reserved, international copyright secured — used by permission of Warner Bros. Publications U.S. Inc., Miami, FL 33014.

"Emotions," lyric and music by Steve Allen; copyright © 1985 EMI / Golden Torch Music Corp. All rights reserved, international copyright secured — used by permission of Warner Bros. Publications U.S. Inc., Miami, FL 33014.

"There's No Way Home," lyric and music by Steve Allen; copyright 1985 EMI / Golden Torch Music Corp. All rights reserved, international copyright secured — used by permission of Warner Bros. Publications U.S. Inc., Miami, FL 33014.

"Keep It from Me," lyric by Steve Allen, music by Larry Cansler; copyright © 1970 Warner-Tamberlane Publishing Corp. and Meadowlane Music Inc. ASCAP. All rights reserved, international copyright secured — used by permission of Warner Bros. Publications U.S. Inc., Miami, FL 33014.

"Houseboat," lyric by Steve Allen, music by George Duning; copyright © 1958, renewed 1986 Famous Music Publishing. All rights reserved, international copyright secured — used by permission.

"Millions and Millions of People," lyric by Steve Allen, music by Marcos Valle; copyright © 1980 Janeiro Music Co. ASCAP. All rights reserved, international copyright secured — used by permission.

"On the Beach" from the motion picture *On the Beach*, lyric by Steve Allen, music by Ernest Gold; copyright © 1959, renewed 1987 Planetary Music Publishing c/o Roulette Records. All rights reserved, international copyright secured — used by permission.

"Cutie Pants," lyric by Steve Allen, music by Ray Brown; copyright © 1964, renewed 1992 Ray Brown Music (BMI). All rights reserved, international copyright secured — used by permission.

Table of Contents

Foreword

by Gene Lees

The expression "Jack of all trades, master of none" seems peculiarly American. Perhaps the saying derives from our faith in the assembly line, where each man specializes in one thing. However, a University of Michigan study some years ago revealed that people with talent in one area may well have it in several.

Our pessimistic maxim would make no sense in Europe, where the cult for specialization does not have the same hold. The Swiss conductor Ernest Ansermet was also a distinguished professor of mathematics. The Russian composer Aleksandr Borodin, who spoke several languages and played piano, flute and cello, was a noted research chemist. The British actor and comedian Dudley Moore, whose degree is in music, is an accomplished pianist and composer. Novelist Anthony Burgess was a respected composer. George Gershwin could well have made his living as a painter; he was that good. The comedian and actor Sid Caesar began life as a saxophonist.

The list of multi-talented people, jacks of all trades and masters of all, is long. I cite it only to emphasize that my friend Steve Allen is not the curiosity he is often seen to be. I must admit, however, that even I am occasionally inclined to shake my head at the protean nature of his abilities.

Steve is one of the most brilliant comedians of our time. If you have seen him on television, which is a restricting medium, you cannot know just how funny he really is. He is at his best on a stage in front of an audience. Then the flow of his verbal improvisations becomes amazing. I don't know how his mind can work that fast. On occasion, when he's in full free-form flight, I find myself wishing he would stop, so I can catch my breath; he reduces everyone in the audience to helpless laughter.

Steve is a good actor, as well as a very good novelist and short story writer. His short stories reveal that he is as inventive in serious narrative forms as he is in improvisational comedy. To date he has published 53 books, fiction and nonfiction alike, with several more at various stages of completion.

Steve is modest about his abilities as a pianist, always citing his admiration for other pianists (above all Erroll Garner), but in fact he is quite good and has recorded a number of well-respected albums. He has a profound knowledge of jazz and admiration for its masters.

And he is an excellent composer and lyricist — two abilities that are rarely found in the same person. There have been only two major composers for American musical theater who wrote both words and music, Cole Porter and Irving Berlin. Most of the best of our songs have come from teams of two, such as Rodgers and Hart, Rodgers and Hammerstein, Lerner and Loewe, and Arlen and Mercer. Steve writes both words and music at a very high level.

But in this volume we are considering primarily his lyrics.

The lyric is the most exacting literary craft I know. I often cite the late French writer—and also trumpet player and lyricist, apropos of versatility—Boris Vian who said he was more proud of his lyrics than his novels. The lyric must meet several criteria that are expected in no other form, including poetry. Long notes require long vowels so that the singer can sustain them. One should, wherever possible, use open vowels (which is to say syllables that do not terminate in consonants), such as *you, too, few, flow, go, know,* at long-note rhyme points, and where this is not possible, use the soft consonants that singers can sustain, as in words such as *dream, seem, rain, plain.* A word should not begin with the same consonant that ended the one preceding it; otherwise you can cause ambiguity of meaning and present the singer with difficulties of execution. Great care must be taken about the vowels used on high notes, avoiding diphthongs wherever possible; diphthongs on high notes present painful problems of pronunciation and can actually push the singer out of tune.

Speech itself is musical. The rises and falls of inflection often convey meaning. Is the statement angry, is it pleading, playful, sad, teasing? All these moods can be conveyed by inflection. For this reason, the matching of lyrics to music is a particularly delicate art, and in ideal instances the melody conforms to what would be the inflections of the words if they were being spoken instead of sung. Conversely, when lyrics are written to an existing melody, the lyricist must be highly sensitive to how they match its contours. Given all these exactions, I rate the craft of the lyric more highly than poetry. Indeed, I think the poets have a lot to learn from the great lyricists.

Not all lyrics can stand alone. Steve has himself satirized the banality revealed in some of them when the deceptive camouflage of music and rhythm are removed. But there are some lyrics that can stand alone, and I cite as examples in this book *This Could Be the Start of Something Big* and the less-known *Collage. Collage* is a startling piece of work, moody and dark, with or without the music.

Most lyricists suffer agonies in the writing process. Occasionally, as Johnny Mercer used to say, you get lucky and a lyric comes easily. For most of us, that luck is rare. But Steve seems to find it often; he writes more easily than anyone I know. Lyrics flow out of him, as do the tunes he so often creates to go with them.

Stephen Valentine Patrick William Allen, to give his full name, was not born in Chicago, as is generally supposed, but in New York City's Harlem, the day after Christmas in 1921. He did, however, grow up in Chicago. He played piano in bands while he was a student at Drake University, later in Phoenix. He became a successful radio entertainer in Los Angeles, then returned to his native city to found the *Tonight* show and become probably the most successful comedian and TV host the medium has ever known. And all the while he championed other musicians, other composers, other comedians. I don't think there is one drop of jealous blood in Steve Allen's body. Perhaps because he is so widely gifted, he is the ultimate appreciator of the talents of others.

I do not know how the circumstances of blood and environment combined to give Steve the vast array of abilities he has. But I'm glad they did.

Gene Lees is a lyricist, composer, singer, musical historian, and author of *The Modern Rhyming Dictionary: How to Write Lyrics.* He is publisher of the highly acclaimed *Jazzletter*, a monthly journal of music.

Preface

As I have prepared this manuscript for publication, and analyzed certain lyrics that I had not even thought of in years, I've realized in how many instances I have addressed a problem that faces lyricists of the present day but which, in a sense, did not even exist in the Golden Age of American music — the 1920s, '30s and '40s. In those days possibilities for wordsmiths were wide open because what it is now possible to see as clichés had not yet established themselves as such. There were always master lyricists, of course, who from the first were cliché-free and whose work was characterized by an innovative freshness and originality. But precisely because they have done so much good work it is now necessary to be even more original in conveying the same old emotional messages that humans have transmitted for untold centuries.

Just the other day in reorganizing some old papers I found that I first addressed this general question in a column I was then doing for *Cosmopolitan* magazine which it seems reasonable to include here.

I have never entirely understood why those curious about the art of song writing so often trouble themselves with the question as to whether lyrics or melodies come first. A perfectly reasonable answer is: who cares? Certainly professional writers do not. Fortunately there is neither a right nor wrong method as regards this simple question. Most of the time I create melodies in the total absence of even a philosophical thought or its articulated rhymed expression. In other cases it is the title and its accompanying lyric that constitute the original grain of sand and in a smaller number of cases it happens that words and music occur simultaneously. This was the case with a song titled "Pretend You Don't See Her, My Heart" which was used as the name of a 1996 novel by Mary Higgins Clark. The number was completed, in just a few minutes, while I was somewhere in Pennsylvania on an east-to-west cross-country drive.

In an even more mysterious case, the main melody and basic lyric message of "This Could Be the Start of Something Big" came to me in a dream, which I was fortunately able to recall when, I assume a few minutes thereafter, I awakened.

Another frequently asked question is: Do song writers create out of the depths of their personal emotional experiences? In other words, is it an actual broken love affair that leads to the creation of a song with a tragic message? On a broad philosophical level, the answer is yes, but as regards most specific numbers, the answer is no. If a composer or lyricist writes, let's say, 100 laments expressing heart-break it by no means follows that he has suffered such a fate 100 times. Once is enough.

Since I have written over 8,000 songs, of which I would think over a thousand have lyrics, it is obvious that the 100 included in this presentation represent only a small percentage of the total. Does it follow that the 100 are simply the best of the lot? Not really.

Actually there doesn't seem, to me, to be a great difference between my best work and that which is of a lower order. If I called in a dozen jurors to make the selections I have no doubt that a dozen separate lists would have been submitted. In some cases my own judgment has probably been affected by the work of the scores of gifted vocalists, arrangers and musicians who have been kind enough to record my material. It may sound odd but when I originally wrote "Impossible," for the score of an early television musical called *The Bachelor*, I had no more regard for it than for any of the other numbers in the show. It was only after hearing such beautiful and emotional performances of the song by Nat Cole, the Hi-Lo's, the King Sisters, Eydie Gorme and others that I began to have a special fondness for it.

A Song Writer Takes the Stand*

(with apologies to Frank Sullivan)

Q: You are a songwriter?
A: *Either that or a tunesmith.*
Q: Try to make your answers direct. Do you write words or music?
A: *Lyrics.*
Q: What do you write most of your songs about?
A: *Love.*
Q: Where do you get your inspiration?
A: *From a voice.*
Q: What kind of voice?
A: *A voice within me.*
Q: Does this voice tell you such things as when you will meet your love?
A: *Yes.*
Q: And when *will* you?
A: *On a night in June.*
Q: Where?
A: *Under the moon.*
Q: Will you recognize your love immediately.
A: *Right from the start.*
Q: What will you notice first about your love? Will you — like other men — look first at her ankles or her trim waist?
A: *No, I will notice her eyes.*
Q: What color will her eyes be?
A: *Blue.*
Q: Why?
A: *Rhymes with "you" and "true."*
Q: How will you address your love?
A: *I'll call her "baby."*
Q: Why?
A: *Rhymes with "maybe."*
Q: What kind of a girl will you consider her?
A: *The* only *girl.*
Q: For whom?
A: *For me.*
Q: Do you consider that this relationship will be one of many?
A: *No, sir.*
Q: Then how long will it last?
A: *Always.*

**First appeared in "Steve Allen's Almanac,"* Cosmopolitan *magazine, November 1956.*

Q: What if the girl is interested in another man?
A: *You mean* … someone else*?*
Q: Precisely. How will you feel?
A: *Blue.*
Q: In that case will your subjective emotional state relate itself to any objective climatic conditions?
A: *Yes, indeed. Take the skies, for example…*
Q: What will the skies be?
A: *They will be cloudy and gray.*
Q: What will you do with yourself if the skies become cloudy and gray?
A: *I will sit in my room.*
Q: What kind of a room is it?
A: *A lonely room.*
Q: Don't you song writers ever live in apartments or houses?
A: *No sir. Only rooms.*
Q: Well, then, where will you make your residence after you marry?
A: *We'll build.*
Q: What will you build?
A: *A little nest.*
Q: How large a nest?
A: *A little nest just meant for two.*
Q: In the event you do get married, who will perform the ceremony?
A: *Parson Brown.*
Q: But if you were Jewish or Catholic…
A: *It makes no difference. All wedding services are performed by Parson Brown.*
Q: But we're putting the cart before the horse. To get back to your love…
A: *My* true *love.*
Q: Limit your replies to direct answers, please. How can you be so sure you'll find such a woman?
A: *I just know that I'll find her.*
Q: When?
A: *Someday. Maybe Tuesday will be my good-news day.*
Q: How do you know?
A: *Somehow. I feel it.*
Q: Where?
A: *Way down deep inside.*
Q: All right. Now suppose you offer this imaginary woman your love. How will you go about it?
A: *I'll take her into my arms.*
Q: You will take her *what* into your arms?
A: *I will take all her charms into my arms.*
Q: And how will she respond?
A: *She will respond with her lips divine.*
Q: What will she do with them?
A: *She will press them close to mine.*
Q: What will be the initial result of this happy circumstance?
A: *Gray skies will turn to blue.*
Q: And what will you be?
A: *Happy again.*

Next witness.

The Lyrics

Collage

As critics have pointed out for over a century, it is unfair to judge song lyrics by standards that properly apply to formal poetry. I naturally refer to true poetry, not greeting-card verse. But on rare occasions lyricists do employ poetic imagery to make their points, and the imagery in "Collage" is of the poetic sort. The genre is usually called that of social protest. Although the number was written in the 1970s, it echoes imagery typical of the usually quiet revolution of the young that took place in the '60s, although some of the concerns expressed are, alas, timeless. Each line of the lyric calls to mind a clear visual picture. If I have worked the effects properly one can almost see a collage of the traditional sort, a collection of photographs from various sources.

On the left-hand wall of my garage
I've got a very strange collage.
It's a crazy jumbled jack-of-all
I've got displayed there on the wall.
Collage,
Collage.

There are pictures torn from magazines
That add up to amazing scenes,
Collage,
My collage.

A bright green sixty-seven Jag,
The blood-stained corner of a flag,
A great big piece of chocolate cake,
A virgin drowning in a lake.
Collage
Collage.

A shiny amber fifth of Scotch,
A lonely soldier standing watch,
A bearded loner smoking dreams,
An ambulance that screams and screams.
Collage
Collage.

A faded stripper on a stage,
An injured baby in a rage,
An empty pointless TV show,
An ancient starving Navajo.
Collage
My collage.

An eight-by-four-by-ten deep freeze,
A black man swinging in the breeze,
Rich ladies in a beauty shop,
Poor people marching till they drop.
Collage,
My collage.

A golden orange rich and round,
A migrant sleeping on the ground,
A mansion and a life of ease,
A closet for the least of these.
Collage,
My collage.

A Klansman looking for a fight,
An orphan boy who cries at night,
A movie star just off to Rome,
Dark windows of an old folks home.
Collage,
My collage.

Three fat men drinking beer from cans,
A young marine who's lost his hands,
A country club that's closed to some,
Sign language for the deaf and dumb.
Collage,
My collage.
Collage.
My collage.

Spring Is Where You Are

The sense of being in a romantic love relationship is, obviously, one of life's supreme delights and brings those who have enjoyed it as close to happiness as they are ever likely to come. But when the lover is deprived of the sight or company of his beloved, the very beauty he misses intensifies the pain of longing or loss. In "Spring Is Where You Are," I deliberately employ poetic metaphors and images by way of emphasizing the beauty of the love relationship.

For whatever reasons spring *is one of the words most commonly employed by poets and, to an even greater extent, by lyricists. The one syllable evokes images of warm blue skies, budding greenery, white clouds, cool breezes and the final retreat of winter and its discomforts. All those who have ever been deeply in love will have become aware that in the absence of the beloved even experiences normally considered delightful are deprived of their full appeal.*

Though the winter snows are thawing,
And the poets hail the Southern star;
The winds of March are unconvincing;
Spring is where you are.
What if robins gaily carol
Symphonies that time can never mar?
Their sweetest songs do not arouse me,
Spring is where you are.

Skies of blue
May do
For other people,

And the sun suffice;
I fear that their philosophy
Will not be
Right for me.

What if all the flowers are blooming,
And their perfume lures me from afar?
My heart ignores their spell and tells me
Spring is where you are.

This Could Be the Start of Something Big

It is a good question whether I can properly take credit for this number at all, given that it occurred to me in a dream. I had been assigned, by producer Joe Cates, to write the score for a musical, The Bachelor, *which was presented on NBC-TV in 1956. Obviously, once the creative portions of my brain had accepted the assignment, they got to work and continued to function whether I was awake or asleep.*

The first seven or eight lines of the lyric were part of the dream, as was the main melody line. Thank goodness I was able to recall that much when I awakened, at which point I made a few handwritten notes. The bridge or alternative melody was created a day or so later. Over one hundred artists, in various parts of the world, have recorded the song during the last four decades.

You're walking along the street,
Or you're at a party,
Or else you're alone and then
You suddenly dig;
You're looking in someone's eyes,
You suddenly realize
That this could be the start of something big!

You're lunching at "Twenty one"
And watching your diet,
Declining a Charlotte Russe,
Accepting a fig;
When out of a clear blue sky,
It's suddenly gal and guy,
And this could be the start of something big!

There's no controlling
The unrolling
Of your fate, my friend,
Who knows what's written in the magic book?
But when a lover
you discover
at the gate, my friend,
Invite her in without a second look!

(continued)

You're up in an aeroplane,
Or dining at Sardi's,
Or lying at Malibu,
Alone on the sand;
You suddenly hear a bell
And right away you can tell,
That this could be the start of something grand.

II

You're doin' your income tax
Or buyin' a toothbrush,
Or hurryin' home because
The hour is late;
Then suddenly there you go,
The very next thing you know,
Is this could be the start of something great!

You're havin' a snowball fight
Or pickin' up daisies.
You're singin' a happy tune,
Or knockin' on wood;
When all of a sudden you
Look up and there's someone new,
Oh, this could be the start of something good!

Your destined lover
You'll discover in a fright'ning flash,
So keep your heart awake
Both night and day,
Because the meeting
may be fleeting as a lightning flash
and you don't want to let it slip away!

You're watching the sun come up,
Or counting your money
Or else in a dim cafe,
You're ordering wine;
Then suddenly there she is,

You want to be where she is,
And this must be a part of something,
This could be the heart of something,
This could be the start of something fine!

You're Something

Everyone who has ever been in love is familiar with the sense that the relevant emotions are so mysteriously powerful that even quite articulate individuals have trouble finding the words to adequately express them. This may be particularly true when one attempts to describe the beloved. In this case, the singer confesses his difficulty, but once he is launched on his attempt he gradually does find appropriate language.

You're something;
I can't find the words, but you're something.
You're magic,
You're flowers, you're sunshine, you're spring.

You're rainbows;
You're children at play in the morning light.
And you're the sky above that I will love
forever.

You're wonder;
You're snow on the trees in the winter.
You're sleigh-bells;
You're music, and perfume, and wine.

You're laughter after tears,
You're prayers an angel hears.
You're leaves of fall
And best of all
you're mine.

Gravy Waltz

As a number of people have pointed out, "Gravy Waltz" is a very peculiar title for a song. I certainly would not have thought of it myself, for the obvious reason that gravy and waltzing have nothing to do with each other. But the title was already established because the melody of the number — written by bassist Ray Brown — had been performed on television and recorded. The challenge, then, was to take two utterly disconnected words and somehow force a relationship between them. The reader may judge from the lyric how successfully this trick was turned.

In 1963, the number received a Grammy award.

I

Pretty mama's in the kitchen this glorious day,
Smell the gravy simmerin' nearly half a mile away.
Lady Morning Glory, I say good mornin' to you,
Chirpy little chickadee told me that my baby was true

Well, she really ran
To get her frying' pan
When she saw me comin'.
Gonna get a taste
Before it goes to waste,
This honeybee's hummin'.

Mister Weepin' Willow, I'm thru
with all of my faults
'Cause my baby's ready to do
The ever-new
Gravy Waltz

How Dare You, Sir?

This number, which has been recorded by Ann Jillian, should be performed at only one-chorus length because it is analogous to a character-sketch, short story, or one-act play, none of which repeat their surprise endings.

The singer, a woman, speaks in a dignified, almost archaic style, but we eventually come to understand that her objections to being addressed, by a stranger in a bar, mask her habituated feelings of loneliness and rejection.

The song is the kind that would be particularly effective in a theatrical musical review.

Meet a long habitue
Of this charming old cafe
Where they know me
The moment I walk in.

Sometimes I dine
At a small secluded table
Or enjoy a glass of wine
At the bar.

I will joke with the gang
If I'm able,
But I must let you know
If you go
too far.

How dare you, sir, address a lady?
By just what right do you presume?
I warn you, sir, do not repeat the offense
Or I will leave the room.

These dim cafes are not my usual haunts;
I've just dropped in to rest awhile.
No one as yet has introduced us.
How dare you, sir, presume to smile?

You say you thought we'd met before somewhere?
Perhaps in Paris or in Rome?
I've heard that line, my pet, before somewhere;
Now I must be getting home.

How dare you, sir, suggest a taxi?
Oh, was it only for yourself?
I thought I sensed an invitation
    but it's plain
    I'll remain
On the shelf.

For now you see a face more lovely, it's true,
At that table for two
By the phone.
Like far too many other men in my life,
How dare you, sir, leave me alone?

I Called Today

The standard repertoire of love-dialogue is, oddly enough, quite limited. Though this seems to pose no problem to those who are in love, it does represent a difficulty for the lyricist who must convey the same ancient messages in ever-new ways. In ages past lovers often communicated by letter. Today the telephone serves the same purpose. "I Called Today" is probably the first song written about that indispensable item, a telephone answering machine.

I called today,
And left a little message.
Called again, And said the same old thing.

My darling, I called today
To tell you I adore you.
I hope it doesn't bore you
With a too-familiar ring.

I felt today
The magic of your fingers,
The sweet perfume
That lingers
    when you've gone.

So have no fear,
For year by year
You can be sure you'll hear—
I called today.

I Think We've Kinda Lost Our Way

Given that the melody, written by band leader/drummer Louis Belson and Jack Hayes, is in the Count Basie ballad groove, it is perhaps odd that the lyric makes a moral point, which is that our rush-rush, hedonistic society tends to overlook the older, simpler, more tender aspects of love.

Lonely lady, sittin' in a singles bar,
Baby, don't you sometimes wonder where
    the good times are?
Hey now, look around;
Don't you think we've kinda lost our way?

I remember when we used to dance like this,
Every summer evening ended with a simple kiss.
Now, wow, what a change!
And I think we've kinda lost our way.

    You can lie
    But you'll cry
    your heart out.
    You can swing
    But you'll sing
    The blues.

    Know the score
    Girl, before
    You start out,
    If you stray
    You will pay
    Your dues.

I can still
Recall the thrill
    of holding hands.
But in recent days
It's all a haze
    of one-night stands.

(continued)

Say, girl, look around;
Get your two feet on the ground.
The day that love comes back to stay
We're gonna find our way
again.

An Old Piano Plays the Blues

I wrote this song in 1948, words and music. Later a then-well-established lyricist, Don George, who had provided words to some of Duke Ellington's jazz melodies, told me he thought he could get Nat Cole to record the song if I would permit a few lyric changes. The deal seemed reasonable, so I allowed George to change a few of the lines. Not only did Nat Cole do the number, but one of the great American songwriters, Hoagy Carmichael, also recorded it.

The clock is striking; guess it must be two.
My baby left me for somebody new.
I've been here playing since she said we're thru.
An old piano plays the blues.

The clock is striking; guess it must be three.
My room is lonely as a room can be.
I'm improvising on a memory—
An old piano plays the blues.

Each ev'ning since we met
We were a close duet
From dusk until the moon would glow low.
And tho' she's gone I find
She's hangin' 'round my mind;
I guess I'm not the kind
to do a solo.

The clock is striking; Lord, it can't be four.
Perhaps I'd better lock the downstairs door.
The one I play for will be here no more—
An old piano plays the blues.

Convince Me

The lyric to "Convince Me" is a fresh way of expressing the insecurity that lovers often feel. And, given that most love relationships do not persist throughout life, the insecurity is understandable. In this case the singer demands that his or her beloved prove that such fears are groundless.

Nature seemed to bless me
With the gift of gab,
And I guess I've used it
Pretty well.

People seem to "yes" me;
No one calls a cab.
They never leave,
Not when I weave
 my spell.

I've won all the arguments,
Always prove my case,
But now there's one I'd really like to lose.
I don't like the things I'm hearing;
Tell me face to face,
There's no reason I should sing the blues.

Convince me,
Be clever if you ever were before.
Convince me I'm wrong about you.
Use every trick you know,
Be slick or slow,
But quick to show
I can't believe what people say.

Convince me,
And show me that I simply must be wrong,
Correct me each step of the way.

Please debate me,
Devastate me,
So I'll know that you don't hate me;
Convince me we're still okay.

Impossible

I dictate these few observations the day after receiving word that Nat Cole's daughter—Natalie—plans to record the song, as her father originally did back in the early 1950s. The number was the love ballad from the NBC television production which also featured "This Could Be the Start of Something Big." It has since been recorded by Andy Williams, The Hi-Lo's, Singers Unlimited, Eydie Gorme, Jennie Smith, Diane Schurr, Jack Jones and a number of other gifted vocalists. The singer is conveying the idea that he had thought he was incapable of establishing a loving relationship but that, thanks to the object of his affections, he has come to realize that what once seemed impossible was now accomplished.

I

If they had ever told me
How sweet a kiss could be,
I would have said, "Impossible,
Impossible for me."

And when they say I'll find love
Beyond the rainbow's end,
I smile and say, "Impossible,
Impossible, my friend."

To dream about what might have been,
Is pointless I agree,
But not as bad as livin, in
A dream I know can never be.

So when they say, "Smooth sailing"
Despite a stormy sea,
I laugh and say, "Impossible,
Impossible for me."

II

When someone tries to tell me
How true a heart can be,
I always say, "Impossible,
Impossible for me."

(continued)

And if they said I'll find you
Beyond the rainbow's end,
I would have said, "Impossible,
Impossible, my friend."

To dream about what might have been,
Is strange enough for me,
But now it seems I'm living in
A dream too beautiful to be.

If they had said a moonbeam
Could calm a stormy sea,
I would have said, "Impossible."
But now at last I see
That nothing is impossible,
If you are here
with me.

Kiss Me with a Smile

This song, too, makes a moral point, which is that sexual expression itself is richer if such subtle emotions are given time to mature.

Kiss me with a smile;
Kiss me from a distance.
Take a little while
To wear down my resistance.

Kiss me with your eyes,
Time enough to touch
And my heart can already feel
so much.

Promise me the moon;
Time enough to reach it.
We've so much to learn
And the stars can teach it.

Love will bring its passion
In a little while,
So for now, my darling
Kiss me with a smile.

Life

It's odd, I suppose, but I had not realized until preparing this collection how often my lyrics express philosophical ideas. This one is consistent with the thinking of Ecclesiastes in the Bible.

Life ... has a way of making fools
Out of those who break the rules
For in time our passion cools
    and we see...

Life is a journey to mysterious heights
    through golden days
    and starry nights.

It seems that life ... is a puzzle to the end.
Is it enemy or friend?
Or a game of let's pretend?
    Who can say?

Love makes it worth the struggle and the strife,
So be it bitter or sweet,
    That's life.

Picnic

Like "Gravy Waltz," "Picnic" is a rather odd title for a song. More commonly there would be some actual thought conveyed by a title rather than the blunt statement of a noun. But in this case, too, I had no choice since the melody had recently been used as the main theme in the 1956 motion picture Picnic, *based on the play by William Inge. Although the McGuire Sisters' vocal helped establish the song as a standard — as did the original film-track instrumental version in which George Duning, the composer, interwove the melody of the old 1930's ballad "Moonglow" — the number has been recorded by several vocalists.*

On a picnic morning
Without a warning
I looked at you
And somehow I knew

On a day for singing
My heart went winging
A picnic grove
Was our rendezvous.

    You and I in the sunshine
    we strolled the fields and farms.
    At the last light of evening
    I held you in my arms.

Now when days grow stormy
And lonely for me
I just recall
Picnic time with you.

Solitaire

One of my favorite people — as both a man and a pianist — was Erroll Garner. A dear fellow, a true genius on his instrument, and a soaringly romantic composer, as his great standard "Misty" makes clear. Erroll used to come to my apartment at 85th and Park in New York and play melodies for me to see if one of them seemed likely to accommodate a lyric. One result was this lovely song, which I entitled "Solitaire," published in 1960.

It was later recorded, quite successfully, by Jerry Vale, who still sings it.

When you're wide awake and lonely
Thru the long and silent night
And your heart won't go to sleep
And so you won't turn off the light;
Then you'll rise once more
And you'll pace the floor ...
And you wait....
      And you wait....
            And you wait.

I'm sitting in my chair
And playing solitaire
And wondering just where
On earth you've gone.

The lazy smoke rings rise
Like dreams before my eyes,
Like dreams I should forget,
Oh, I know I should and yet...

Your face comes back to me
The way it used to be
When love was very new
And hearts were careless, too.
Now nothing's left at all.
The blinding teardrops fall
As I recall you.

I know that very soon
The solitary moon
May be the only company for me.

Oh, somewhere in the night,
Where lights are burning bright
And other lips are free
Then do you ever think of me?

The whisper of the rain
Can never soothe the pain,
For it's oh, so very, very hard to bear.

So tho' the hour is late,
I sit alone and wait.
You left me playing
sol-i-taire.

The South Rampart Street Parade

"The South Rampart Street Parade" is, I believe, the greatest Dixieland classic of them all. Lest that sound conceited, given that I wrote the lyric, I must explain that I'm talking about the original instrumental performance by the Bob Crosby orchestra of the 1930s. Ray Bauduc and Bob Haggart of Crosby's rhythm section are credited with the melody, which led me once to ask Bauduc and Haggart who actually wrote the different parts of the song, given that it has eight quite distinct melodies and is, in fact, the longest popular song ever written.

"To tell the truth," Ray said, "we're not really sure. In fact we're not even sure we created any of the number because all the licks seemed like things we heard the old Dixieland bands play when we were growing up."

Since in this case, too, the title was already established, my task, as lyricist, was relatively simple. I simply had to describe one of the old New Orleans Dixieland street parades.

I used to love the Crosby band when I was a kid, in Chicago, and got into the Blackhawk Club once or twice to hear the group in person. What a kick.

I don't know why it took me so long to ask if a lyric had ever been done for the number, but it didn't occur to me until about 1951, by which time CBS had moved me to New York to do television.

I've written a boxcar full of lyrics but that was the toughest one, oddly enough because at first I was trying to write words as the melody notes flew by.

I finally realized I was working unnecessarily hard when it occurred to me I could play the 78 RPM record at 33⅓. At that point the whole thing sounded like a tuba solo but at least I was able to hear the separate notes more easily. Believe it or not, I had a hell of an argument with the publisher — was it Robbins, Feist and Miller? — in New York. The head man — I think his name was Lester Sims — said "This is terrific lyric, but it'll never make it in the pop market as a vocal. Why don't you just cut it down to one *of the melodies and then use maybe another one for the bridge?"*

I realized that while I could have acted on his suggestion it would have been really dumb to do so since the tune is a true masterpiece as is.

In any event, after the publisher wised up he took a copy of my lyric with a demo vocal where I sang over the Bob Crosby recording. I had no idea what he was doing with it so it was quite a surprise when, several weeks later, I got a call from Tom Mack, who was in charge of Decca Records on the West Coast. He told me he had a little surprise for me, but didn't want to tell me what it was. He wanted me to come over to his studios to hear it. Of course I got over there as fast as possible.

It was one of the real thrills of my life hearing Bing and the Andrews Sisters do that vocal version. I don't know myself who did the arrangements, but it retained the excitement of the original instrumental and knocked me out entirely.

Do you hear the beat,
Away down the street?
Do you hear the neat
    Little rhythm
    Of the happy dancin' feet?

Well, now,
Look there!
The people are runnin',
And right now,
They're gonna have a lot of fun.

Make way,
'Cause everybody's comin,
And you'll see a big parade.

Hey, boy, you're really gonna celebrate,
Hear that?
Listen to the clarinet.
Your feet are really gonna palpitate
When you are marchin' around.

Marchin' around
Wonderful sound,

I hear the rattle-de-tat;
I love to hear the way the little drummer does that.
Oh, what a glorious day,
Out o' my way!
Make room and gimme some air;
I got a little rhythm to spare!

(continued)

We all swing high,
Swing low,
Everybody rockin'
To and fro.
It ain't fast
Or slow
But oh,
That glory hallelujah!
Swing that thing
Make the river bottom ring
And sing.
Hush ma mouth,
That's the South
 Rampart Street Parade!

They're doin' it,
Soft shoein' it,
They're tryin' it,
Untyin' it.

They're jivin' it,
Revivin' it,
I tell you.

They're struttin' it,
Rug-cuttin' it,
They're shakin' it,
And breakin' it,
Hey, Dad!
Not bad!
I'm glad
You dig!
Hey, boy—

Every boy's got a girl,
The town's gonna whirl,
Tonight's a jamboree,
Mister, and if you come along
You'll join in the song.
Hey, Dad!
Not bad!
I'm glad
You dig!
Hey, boy that
Band is grand,

Everybody in the land's
On hand.
They demand
That brand
of dand-y
Handy Dixieland.

The way
They play
Makes a body want to stay
All day.

Hush ma mouth,
It's the South
Rampart Street Parade!

I hear the trombone, la-de-ah-de-ah,
That shiny trombone, la-de-ah-de-ah.
Everybody playin' mighty fine as they march along,
And I never get enough of that Creole song!

Hear now, la-de-ah-de-ah
It's loud and clear now, la-de-ah-de-ah.
I really get a thrill,

I know I always will,
Whenever I can hear the rhythm of a band.

Way down yonder in the cane break,
You can hear the music they make,
Ringin' out until the daybreak.
Louisiana band,
Gotta get a hand.
It's the South
Rampart Street Parade!

Oh, How Slow

This lyric concerns the tendency of strong emotions to distort our perception of time. Ten seconds of excruciating pain seems an eternity. Ten seconds in the presence of one's beloved seems over in an instant.

Oh, how slow
The lonely moments go
Because the gods said no,
    it could not be.

Oh, how gray
The colors of my day,
With spring as far away
    as you from me.

I know there's nothing in my life
    worth living for,
    now that love has flown.
Oh, how wrong
The notes of ev'ry song
    we've ever known.

Oh, how fine
When you were daily mine
And all of life's design
    was right and true.

Oh, how warm,
When ev'ry dream took form
    before our eyes.

It seems only yesterday we touched
But we had much
    to learn.
Oh, how fervently I pray
    for your return.

Theme from Bell, Book and Candle

Bell, Book and Candle *was the title of a 1958 film for which Columbia's resident motion picture scorer George Duning wrote the background music. In this case, too, I was "stuck with" the title and obviously had to write a lyric about witchcraft, an imaginary fantasy with which mankind has from time to time either amused or horrified itself.*

These I require to call you forth—
Bell, book and candle.
Here by the fire and facing north,
I'll work my magic on you.

Midnight will start the witching hour,
Hour of enchantment,
Then I'll impart the mystic power
Humans believe is taboo.

There are those who laugh at witchcraft
But they've never been caught in its glow.
At the sound of the bell
You are under my spell
You'll be trapped by the voodoo that I do.

Silence the bell and close the book.
Snuff out the candle.
Witchcraft was just a chance I took
Too hot to handle,
Bell, book and candle,
I'm only human with you.

Cold

This lyric was written for a strong and quite original country-style melody by Larry Cansler, though some of its imagery is more poetic than is customary for that genre.

Cold, it was a-mighty cold
Cold as the heart of someone who doesn't love you.
I remember that
Cold, it was a-freezin' cold,
Cold as the look in eyes that no longer love you.

Anybody can feel
When it's gettin' late
Too late for goin' back to a happy summer.,
When the winter is here
And you're all alone
All you can do is pray that it's gettin' warmer.
Once upon a time there was sunlight and mornin'-glory,
Bluebirds in the blue up above me,
Then you told me you didn't love me.
Down I crashed like an eagle struck by lightning,
Thought that I was makin' it my way.
Now I walk the cold, lonely highway.

Blue. I was a-mighty blue.
Blue as the eyes that look at me so unseeing.
I'm a-tellin' you, down, down at the end of town,
Down where the papers blow, well, I'm also fleeing.
Cold, it's been a-mighty cold
Cold as the lonely world that we all were born in.

Cold, it's been a-freezin' cold,
Cold as the frozen sun of this winter mornin'.

Emotions

(*From* Alice in Wonderland)

"Emotions" is a sweet ballad written for the score of Alice in Wonderland, *the CBS-TV Irwin Allen production for which I provided the film's 19 songs. In it the Red Queen, played by Ann Jillian, explains to little Alice why humans behave as unpredictably and irresponsibly as they often do.*

ALICE:
Is life just a giant game of chess?

THE RED QUEEN:
I assure you, the answer is "yes!"

ALICE:
Do you mean that something is moving us about?

THE QUEEN:
That's for me to know and you to find out.

Is the ocean as level as a pool?
To think so you'd have to be a fool.
There are millions of waves in an ocean,
So something obviously keeps them all in motion.

And do you stand motionless, my girl?
No, you constantly are running in a whirl,
But since you've come, uninvited, for this visit
I should think that you'd

Be wond'ring—
What is it?

Should I reveal to you the secret, my dear?

ALICE:
Yes, your majesty. That's what I'd like to hear.

THE QUEEN:
When the world seems full of trouble and of strife,
What moves us through this crazy game of life?

(continued)

Emotions, emotions.
They're much stronger than magical potions.
They make us behave as we do.
You may like it or not, but it's true.

Emotions, emotions,
When we smile or we frown, that is why.
Some are good, some are bad,
Some are sweet, some are sad.
Can't escape them, however we try.
We've emotions, my dear, till we die.

The Final Curtain

"The Final Curtain," which may be taken to mean either death or the last chapter of any specific venture, not necessarily theatrical, was at one time part of the score of the 1963 Broadway musical Sophie. *It proved to be so depressing, however, that we decided to take it out of the show.*

I finally used it, sometime later, when one of my television series reached the end of its course.

The final curtain
One day will fall for certain
So when it does just bow very low
And close up the show
    that day.

Did they applaud you?
It may have overawed you,
But keep in mind the curtain must fall
once and for all
    some day.

    And though your heart is breaking
    You'll just have to cry alone
    'Cause, mister, they've got troubles of their own.

The final curtain
One day will fall for certain
And when it does it's one of those things;
Just head for the wings
    to stay.

The final curtain must fall
    some fine day.

Laugh

(*From* Alice in Wonderland)

Anthony Newley was not only a personal friend but one of my favorite entertainers. I could watch him on stage for hours, so unique a performer was he. It was therefore an honor indeed to be able to create this song for him, which he performed as The Mad Hatter.

THE MAD HATTER:
Laugh—at ev'ry single thing we do.
Just laugh, and we shall all perform for you.
Just smile and tensions will unwind
    And you'll find
    that your mind
    takes a kinder
        view.

Laugh—Yes, even when your skies are gray.
Just laugh, and troubles seem to float away.
You'll find it's very true, my dears,
    Through the years
    that your tears
    and your fears
        will fly.

Oh, there are times when crying
    seems the thing to do,
But keep on trying
    till your dreams come true.
Your heart, I'm sure, knows what is best for you,
So laugh, little girl, just laugh.

When Stella's in the Room

(*For Stella Adler*)

This lyric was written as a tribute to a special person, the late Stella Adler. To the moment of her death, in late 1992, well into her 80s, she was a grand and glamourous figure of the American theater, one whose work had influenced some of our major actors.

The song, which had been performed at a number of public functions during Ms. Adler's later years, was also sung at her memorial tribute.

When Stella's in the room
Nobody else shines quite as bright,
And Stella's in the room tonight
So marvel at her glow.

She'll turn and smile at you,
But not as others do,
And for that moment you'll
    know love.

When Stella's in your sight, ah, then
You'll dream about what might have been;
You'll think about another fate;
But you're too late,
    idle dreamer.

So there she stands, my friends;
Shall we drink another toast?
To Stella—
The one we love the most.

I Depend on Me

(*The Prostitute's Song*)

There has been very little music written, over the centuries, about prostitution, for reasons that are understandable enough. It's a profession to which men are driven only out of desperation and even in our anything-goes age the practitioners of the trade are, sad to say, looked down upon. Cole Porter's "Love for Sale" dealt with the subject, but in Porter's customarily brilliant and witty way. In writing the score for the musical The Al Chemist Show *(presented in 1980 by the Los Angeles Actors' Theatre), which was based on Ben Jonson's* The Alchemist, *I thought it was time to write a realistic number about women who are reduced to renting their bodies. The song was performed in the show by the gifted English entertainer Georgia Brown. Ann Jillian has also done an excellent recording of it. Note that, far from glamorizing the profession, the song deals with it in a very straightforward and tragic way.*

Once again, on the rocks,
Once again, out of luck, in danger
Once again, to the gods a stranger.

Why?
Must it be that I
Am condemned, like Sisyphus, to repeat my fate?

If I pray
From the blue, no answer.
No strong partner for this poor dancer;
But that's fine
For I'm not inclined
To become resigned.

When I've got a friend
Who will see me through
To the bitter end.

When I was six years old—
I was kicked out in the cold
And it taught me I'd look out—
for myself.

Me—that's who I depend on.
Nobody else gives a damn
Who I am
Or what garbage dump I end on.

To this very day,
Mister, I pay my own way
And good luck to those who play
By the rules.

Tough! That's what life is,
No sweet land of milk and honey;
Rough! That's what life is,
And worse, if you've got no money.

So I do what I must to survive, you see,
I've been burned
And I've learned
I can only depend on me!

When I was just so high—
And I spread my wings to fly
I was slapped down as if I—
Were a bug.

So, me—that's who I can turn to.
Not some stupid John who I con
In the hay;
in the way
I've learned to.

In the days ahead
On the street or in some bed
Day or night I shake my fist
At the sky.

Tough! That's what life is,
As cruel as a wild piranha.
Rough! That's what life is,
No heaven and no nirvana.

So I do what I must to survive, you see
I've been burned
And I've learned
I can only depend on me.

Hello, Goodbye (That's Life)

This song-poem, written for a lovely melody by Michael Leonard, was somewhat more difficult to write than would ordinarily be the case, because the separate musical phrases that comprise the tune were all quite short, consisting, in fact, of only four notes, which meant that they could be matched to just four syllables. The lyric lists experiences classic to our individual predicament in a difficult world.

Hello, good-bye.
We laugh, we cry.
We're born, we die.
    That's life.

We smile, we frown.
We're up, we're down.
We're star or clown.
    That's life.

We're thrilled or bored.
Despised, adored.
We're slave or lord.
    That's life.

We freeze, we burn.
We stand, we turn.
We live and learn
    That's life.

All that you can do
Is try to muddle through,
And to yourself be true,
    My friend.

We work, we play,
We're sad or gay.
What can we say?
    That's life!

We're foe, or friend.
We save, we spend.
But in the end
      That's life.

Yes, in the end
That's life!

Your Wife Is the Love of My Life

A few years after my friend Johnny Mercer (also my favorite lyricist) died, television producer Bill Harbach brought to me a song title which Johnny's widow Ginger had found among his personal papers. Bill thought, quite properly, that such a marvelously dramatic title should not simply go to waste. He and Ginger were kind enough to ask if I would be interested in converting it into a song.

In doing so I simply developed the plot line the title implies. The singer is addressing a man he considers more fortunate than himself, and he strongly hopes that the lucky fellow appreciates his good fortune.

VERSE:
In case they've never told you,
You're a very lucky man.
Now, I don't mean to scold you,

But believe me, chum, I can,
If you don't appreciate the girl you married.
For very long ago
She told me, "Thanks, but no."

We've never met since then
But I remember when—

CHORUS:
Your wife
Is the love of my life,
But the love of my life had other ideas.
Those eyes, that you see ev'ry day
So familiar they may
Not seem as lovely as they are.

One sigh,
Then she kissed me goodbye;
So I hope you appreciate
Your happy fate,
My friend.

Her smile
And her fabulous style,
They were mine for awhile,
But that's how it goes.
As most everyone knows
Your wife was the love of my life.

After You

The separation of two people who actually love each other inevitably brings a sadness so common a part of the human predicament as to be classic. At such times our concentration is often on ourselves and the pain we are personally feeling. At other moments it is the lost love that is concentrated upon. Even after such moments of tragedy, and sometimes the passage of a great deal of time, it generally does become possible to become emotionally involved with someone else, but in the case of this lyric the singer perceives such a future as unlikely at best because of the near-perfection of the one who has been lost. This haunting melody was written by Jennie Smith.

After you,
After you,
What could warm me
After you?

Not the sun,
Not the flame,
After you.

After spring,
Could we know
Any season with its glow?

What could matter
To my heart
After you?

Kings could bring from afar
Golden laughter in a jar;
I'd only show them strings of tears like pearls.

You were life,
You were love
You were blessings from above;

There can be
Nothing new,
Not for me,
After you.

The Time of My Life

The singer, in delivering this particular message, looks back over a long, full and fortunate life in which he has enjoyed the blessings of an extended love relationship.

I've had the time of my life.
Oh, yes. The time of my life.
I guess—things never could be
So lovely for me
again.

You were the belle of the ball;
I was the king of them all.
No other man could dispute my claim.
Tell me you felt the same.

I had the time of my life
For sure—the time of my life
And you're the reason and rhyme
That I've had the time I've had.

And now with all of my life in view,
I'll pray, as I often do,
That I can spend
All the time of my life with you.

Nice Little Girls

In today's depraved society the very concept of Nice Little Girls sounds quaint, a relic of an earlier and more civilized time.

The number of adults is proportionately what it ever was, but the number of ladies and gentlemen is now so low as to literally endanger the continuance of a civilized society.

Nice little girls
Never are unkind.
Nice little girls
Leave the past behind,
But nice little girls
Sometimes lose their mind,
Nice little girls like me.

Nice little girls
Never strive to win.
Through rain or shine
Keep a cheerful grin,
But nice little girls
Take it on the chin–
Yes, little girl; you'll see.

The golden rule still rules me
And I turn the other cheek.
And yet the finish often fools me;
I don't feel so blessed being meek.

Nice little girls
In their shiny shoes,
Nice little girls
Always pay their dues,
But nice little girls
Often get the blues.
You don't call
And we're all
at sea,
Nice little girls like me.

The Things My Heart Tells Me

The old expression Love is blind *actually represents a fragment of a larger and more disturbing truth. The fact is that all the emotions are blind. Of love there will never be enough in the world, but its seeds fall as haphazardly as those of the wilderness. Even in those lone individuals who are distinguished by the strength of their will, the rational powers are often overruled by the desires of the heart.*

I tell my heart I'm better off without you,
That I must somehow set you free,
But then I dream and in the night
you should hear
The things my heart tells me.

I tell my heart to nevermore adore you,
Our love just wasn't meant to be,
But when the lights go out you
really should hear
The things my heart tells me.

What do I want from life?
I ask my heart
To tell me true.
What am I looking for?
The answer's always "you."

I tell my heart that I'll go on without you
If that's the fate the stars decree
But then I close my eyes and
you ought to hear
The things my heart tells me.

I Love You Today

This romantic ballad, also part of the score of Sophie, *expresses an emotion common to those who are truly in love. Presumably they have already revealed the fact of their feeling, but they predict that the current strength of their love will persist.*

This song has been recorded by Kathie Keegan, Marilyn Maye and Jennie Smith, among others.

Good morning, my dear,
I love you today.
I've said it before, I know,
But even so,
I love you today.

The tree in the meadow
The lark in the blue
Will see the lovely fire
  of my desire
  for you.

Hello there, my friend,
I love you today.
My heart wants to draw a crowd,
And sing out loud,
I love you today.

One life won't be long enough,
My love to convey;
So just you wait and see,
Through all eternity,
These words you'll hear from me,
I love you today.

Beautiful Women

This lyric represents a conscious attempt to make a moral statement. It does not deny the obvious-enough fact that we are genetically, naturally programmed to be impressed by the beauty of others, but it still holds out the ideal of limiting our sexual and romantic attentions to one.

Nature gave us flowers,
Waterfalls and trees.
We are blessed with winds and springtime,
Rivers, pools, and seas.
Blue skies and mountains,
Gardens in the sun,
Sunsets and starry night;
Wonders, every one.
But–
Beautiful women,
Ah, what a gift!
Beautiful women
Make the heart lift.

Beautiful women,
Gracing the earth,
Lovely as lilies;
Treasure their worth.

We can enjoy all the flowers.
All of us own the sun,
But as for beautiful women
We must select but one.

Beautiful women
Smiling and free,
Blazing in glory
For you and me.

Dream of their faces,
Glow at their charms,
Beautiful women,
Here in our arms.

(continued)

Voices of music,
Forward or shy.
Beautiful women,
Pleasing the eye.

Beautiful women,
All colors and heights
Cheering our mornings,
Warming our nights.

We may climb all the mountains,
Accumulate much of their gold.
Ah, but of women there'll be just one
To have,
To hold.

See how they walk now,
Sweet with perfume
Singing like April,
Warming a room.

Beautiful women
God, how they shine!
That one is yours, man,
This one
Yes, this one
Is mine.

One Little Thing

The lyric to this ballad is, I concede, totally depressing. Whether mother nature designed it so or not, the fact is that not only do love relationships sometimes go wrong, they do so far more often than they go right.

During a lifetime the average person may have the sense of being in love perhaps ten times. But except in societies in which polygamy is common, we consider ourselves fortunate if one such relationship — the last one — persists. In fact, the early heart-breaks might be said to be training and preparation for that one that leads to marriage and is, one hopes, the last we experience.

Songs in which the singer boasts of the degree of his happiness are scarce, and if there are a few such, for every one of them there must be at least a hundred in which the speaker bemoans his fate.

In any event, the message of "One Little Thing" is that the lover is attempting to keep his courage up.

I've discovered, in performing the number, that the line that suddenly quiets the audience and concentrates its attention is the one that comes at the end of the verse, "I may — die."

All right
You're gone.
What's done is done.
We both could read the signs,
But the only problem is
I forget my lines.

I'll get along.
I did before I met you
Now that I have let you
    get away.

I've got things all figured out,
Telling you
No lie.
There's just one little problem:
I may die.

    How—do I get through the night?
    And how
    Will I live through tomorrow?
    And how

(continued)

About the rest of my life?
Other than that
Things'll be fine.

Now
When I listen to music,
And now
When the telephone rings
And there's not enough of me
to answer,
Won't that be a scream?

A scream,
A *scream*
That you'll never hear
Because I love you much too much.

It's strange how everything here
Still seems to tremble at your touch.
I'll be all right

But how
Do I hide from the storm?
Oh, wow! It was cozy and warm
With you here in my arms,
All that wonderful spring.
I'm fine,
But how do I live?
There's just that one little thing.

After Awhile

"After Awhile," written to a haunting melody by Jennie Smith, expresses emotions with which, sad to say, almost everyone becomes familiar at some point during his or her life's course. The time-setting is after the collapse of an important love relationship; the singer is expressing the hopeful sentiment that he will eventually recover from his current depression. And precisely when might that period of recovery begin? "After awhile ... only ten thousand years."

After awhile
I'll be well,
I'll be strong.

After awhile,
Tho' the night
May be long,
dear.

There'll come a day
When the flowers green will grow.
After awhile,
This I pray,
This I know.

Now your smile
No longer lights my sky.
Now the wind
Is cold, and so am I.

But after awhile
No more pain,
No more tears.
After awhile
We'll forget all our fears.
After awhile:
Only ten thousand years.

I Hate New York

This semi-comic lyric is based on the often-heard condemnation of New York City, which was once a far more civilized community than it is at present. And yet, even on the part of armies of New Yorkers who daily criticize the old town, there is still a deep affection for it and an appreciation of its specific virtues and attractions.

VERSE:
Laugh it up, folks,
These are the jokes.
Our city is falling apart.

You kick it around
Now that it's down.
I haven't got the heart.

Oh, I know that there's plenty that's wrong,
But why do I still
Feel that old thrill
At any old familiar
New York song?

CHORUS:
I hate New York,
Except for Broadway op'ning nights,
The magic of those twinkling lights,
The Garden and those crazy fights,
I hate New York.

I hate New York,
Except for Sundays in the Park,
The Hudson River in the dark,
The way you call me on a lark,
I hate New York.

That sky-line
Still does me in.
Even Mr. Kempton's byline
Makes me know
What state I'm in.

I hate this town,
Except for bike-rides in the sun,
Lunch with the bunch at "21,"
A small cafe when day is done.

I've panned it,
Can't stand it.
I hate New York.

You May Have Been Loved Before

The singer makes so bold, in this lyric, as to do the equivalent of Al Jolson's famous line, when he followed a line-up of the superstars of his day, "You ain't heard nothin' yet."

If the object of his love is more than a very young teenager, it is likely the case that she has been loved or desired by others. But the singer's confidence makes him assert that so far as satisfying the young lady's requirements are concerned, her past experience will pose no difficulties by comparison.

You—may have been loved before,
But I will love you more.
More than the rest,
More than the best
you've known.

You—may have been thrilled before,
But I will thrill you more.
Wait and see,
You're gonna be
surprised.

I won't need a soft guitar to strum.
Just one kiss, and you'll hear a soft insistent drum.

So—though you're blase, my pet
You ain't seen nothin' yet.

You may have been loved before
But I will love you more.

Strawberry Wine

This song-poem, which I provided for a lovely melody by Jeff Harris, is written in a purposely old-fashioned English manner. The imagery is strongly poetic.

Strawberry wine,
Thistledown honey,
Springtime is selling her sweets in the lane.
Who will decline
Goldenrod money?
Springtime is handing it out once again.

So finders keepers.
Losers weepers.

Strawberry wine,
Blueberry candy,
Springtime is giving it freely away.
Let us recline
On anything handy.
April is treating us warmly today.

The Things We Never Got to Do

We will probably never know how many songs about lost love have been written, but their very number does pose a challenge for lyricists, one that I believe, in this instance, has been adequately responded to. The message of the lyric is that it is normal for the disappointed lover to miss whatever was beautiful and productive in a past relationship, but that his present sense of loss is so extreme that he even misses — longs for — things that probably would have been inevitable but which now will never happen because the love affair has ended.

VERSE:

Everyone has memories, for love brings more than its share.
You and I have memories too painfully lovely to bear,
But there's more reason for my sorrows
For lately I've been dreaming of those
    ever-lost tomorrows.

CHORUS:

The things we never got to do
Will haunt me all the long years thru,
My darling.

The things we never got to say
Will haunt me ev'ry lonely day
    to come.
The wine we never got to taste,
The time we never got to waste
    I remember.

The plans we never got to make,
The trips we never got to take
    I regret.
That honeymoon we dreamed about
And now will have to do without
    I long for.

My dear, somewhere along the way
The best-laid plans can go astray
    It seems.

So it's no wonder, precious friend,
Those years we never got to spend
Make the tear-drops fall.
I wonder if you miss them too,
The things we never got to do
    at all.

Where's My Dream?

Life is generous to some of us, and stingy to others, there being no natural justice or fairness in the daily workings of the vast universe. Some of us ultimately realize at least a few of our early dreams and hopes; others are not so fortunate. The singer here recalls the dreams of his youth but now wonders what has gone wrong in the development of them.

When I was a very little child
Looking at the clouds could make me dream.
            Now—that the world is older,
            Now—when the wind is colder,
Where's my dream?

Later, when I was a boy in school,
Lying in the grass beside the stream,
      Oh, how I dreamed of someone;
      Oh, how I needed someone.
Where's my dream?

      I have done important things,
      So some people say.
      They're not such important things,
      When winter skies are gray.

I remember laughing in the sun
A million years ago—at 21,
Now, though I'm lord and master,
      Time turns forever faster.
Where's my dream?

There's No Way Home

(***From*** **Alice in Wonderland**)

This was written in a moment of minor irritation while I was providing the 19 songs that eventually comprised the score of the two-night television production of Alice in Wonderland. *I had written two other numbers for the Cheshire Cat (played by Telly Savalas) to sing to little Alice when she is lost in the woods. But producer Irwin Allen said he did not want a playful approach but rather something somber, even threatening.*

"All right," I thought, without expressing my reaction to Irwin. "You want threatening? You'll get it, and in spades." The lyric suggests not only that Alice will never find her way back to her original home but that this is consistent with the fate of humanity in the vast universe generally.

There's no way home from this strange land.
Don't even try to understand.
You're lost in time, without a trace.
Resign yourself to your disgrace.

Somehow you've strayed, and lost your way,
And now there'll be no time to play.
No time for joy, no time for friends,
Not even time to make amends.

You are too naive
If you do believe
Life is innocent
    laughter and fun.
There are things to fear
So you see, my dear,
Your adventures have only begun.

The world's immense, but sad to say,
It makes no sense in any way.
So what care I
If you should cry?
There's no way home.

Keep It from Me

(*A boy to his father*)

This unusual number is designed to be sung by a teenager to his generally inattentive father. It expresses anger but, at an even deeper level, the sadness that is always felt by those whose parents do not properly administer to their needs, particularly the emotional. The boy refers to the parent's own inadequacies, which leads to his own anger and resentment, but still concedes that behind the anger he wishes, even now, that his relationship with his father had been closer and warmer.

Is there something you would like to give,
Something that you think would help me live
    The good life,
    Free of all strife?

Well, old-timer,
Maybe you had better keep it to yourself now.
    Keep it from me, old-timer
    'Cause it didn't do you too much good,
    Didn't help you do the things you should,
    Didn't make you mind the Golden Rule,
    Didn't stop you bein' might fool-
        ish at times,
How 'bout those times, old-timer?
I remember how you came home all in a rage,
    Actin' your age,
    Old-timer.

So I hope that you will understand
When things don't turn out the way you planned.

Still—I dream of the nights you were away, man.
Oh, then—
I used to pray
Somehow somewhere, someday.
Now I fear that it's too late, old man.
What you did was better teaching than
    You could see.
    Keep it from me,
    No hard feelin's.

Gonna build a better world tomorrow, my friend
Sorrow may end
a little bit,
But at least, old man, we're gonna try,
And we're not afraid to laugh and cry.
Gotta stretch our wings and learn to fly.
Lord, you have to live
before you die.

The Loveliest Garden That I've Ever Seen

(*From* Alice in Wonderland)

"The Loveliest Garden That I've Ever Seen" was written for the CBS-TV production of Alice in Wonderland, *although it was eventually cut out of the production simply because there wasn't room for it.*

Given that the story of Alice *is from the English culture of the last century, the lyric is written more in the English idiom than the American.*

It's the loveliest garden that I've ever seen;
It's ever so sunny, and ever so green,
With rows of pink roses
To tempt all our noses,
Cool water from mountains
All splashing in fountains.

The loveliest garden in all of the land,
Completely enchanting, and ever so grand.

Its trees are so shady,
Some fortunate lady
Could walk with a parasol lightly in hand.
It's all so refreshingly clean.
The nicest and neatest
And certainly sweetest
Garden that I've ever seen.

Oh, That Face

Except for those who are sightless, it is usually the face of the partner that is idealized and loved, among her various physical attractions. The young woman in question may, in fact, be deemed by even the disinterested as strikingly beautiful, but even when she is not, the lover contrives to see something in her face that seems beautiful to him, if only because of possible resemblances to his idealized vision of his mother.

Oh, that face!
There's something about it,
I just have to shout it
    out.

Oh, those eyes.
There's something about them;
I can't do without them,
    my love.

    It's been quite a while
    Since I saw such a smile
    And, in fact, I guess I never did.
    I've been bowled over,
    My heart just rolled over
    The moment we met.
    Now I can't forget.

Oh, that face,
And if I should kiss it
I know that I'd miss it
    forever.

So please keep it near me,
To thrill me, to cheer me;
Oh, that face!

If You Were My Baby All the Time

This number, which falls somewhere between country-and-western and pop-ballad, is, of course, a love song, but one which expresses chiefly the singer's regret that there is something standing in the way of the perfect happiness he believes might be his if only he and his beloved were truly one, in every common sense.

If you were my baby all the time,
Oh, yeah.
If you were my baby all the time
You'd never have to earn a dime;
Oh, no,
'Cause I'd love you so.

When you'd awake at dawn
I never would be gone;
I'd smile at your sweet head on the pillow.

If you did something wrong
I'd never scold you.
If you did something wrong
I just would hold you.

You'd see;
That's how it would be.
If you were my baby all my life,
Oh, God–

If you were my baby all my life
If we were a simple man-and-wife,
You'd see–
How sweet it would be.

When I'd come home at night
And see your smile so bright
I'd be the richest man in the world.

If you were seein' storm clouds up above you
To keep you safe and warm I just would love you.
If you were my baby
    all the time.

Pretend You Don't See Her, My Heart

This simple waltz, in the Italian style, was written about an actual failed love affair, early in my life. It was conceived and finished, in a few minutes, while I was driving across country alone.

The number turned out to be a hit for Jerry Vale, who still occasionally performs it, and did so not long ago in the 1990 motion picture Goodfellas, *about New York City Mafia life.*

Pretend you don't see her,
My heart,
Although she is coming our way.

Pretend you don't need her,
My heart,
Just smile and pretend to be gay.

It's too late for running,
My heart.
Chin up
If the tears start to fall.

Look somewhere above her,
Pretend you don't love her,
Pretend you don't see her at all.

Houseboat

This title — like "Picnic" and "Gravy Waltz" — is one I would never have devised. But the one-word title had to be kept simply because the melody was the main theme of the 1958 motion picture Houseboat, *which starred Cary Grant and Sophia Loren. But something about the sweet melody, by film composer George Duning, appealed to me and what might have been a somewhat limiting title proved, in fact, to pose no difficulty at all. All I had to do was describe an idyllic setting in which the two lovers float downstream, on peaceful waters, on an actual houseboat.*

There's a houseboat
Driftin' down the river;
It's a palace,
If you're there with me.

Life is easy
Driftin' down the river;
Summer calls us
Where the wind is free.

The hummingbird is drinkin'
The honeysuckle wine
And flirtin' with the turtle dove;

And if the thoughts you're thinkin'
Are anything like mine,
Then this could be a night of endless love.

Time was when I
Dreamed of greener pastures;
Then I met you and now I see
What's best for me:
A houseboat just for two.

Cool Yule

This is one of the few comic lyrics included in the present collection. Yule is, obviously, an ancient English word meaning Christmas, and cool is part of the jazz musician's urban street lingo, which originated in the early 1930s. The fact that the two words rhyme facilitated my task.

The number was first recorded in 1953 by the immortal Louis Armstrong, who seemed able to bring a lightly comic touch to almost everything he recorded, especially as a vocalist.

From Coney Island to the Sunset Strip,
Somebody's gonna make a happy trip
 tonight,
While the moon is bright.

He's gonna have a bag of crazy toys,
To give the gonest of the girls and boys,
So, dig!
Santa comes on big!

 He'll come a-callin' when the snow's the most,
 When all you cats are sleepin' warm as toast.
 And you are gonna flip when old St. Nick
 Plays a lick
 On a peppermint stick!

He'll come a flyin' from a higher place
And fill the stockin's by the fireplace,

 So you'll
 Have a Yule
 that's cool!

Oh, What a Night for Love

"Oh, What a Night for Love," a classic from the Count Basie book from the 1950s, was written to accommodate a beautiful, lulling melody by the gifted composer/arranger Neil Hefti. I chose to develop the lyric's storyline by connecting a list of precise and poetic nature-images.

The number has been recorded and performed by Ella Fitzgerald and Mel Torme, among other jazz specialists.

A strawberry moon,
Blueberry sky,
Polka dot stars
Shinin' on high;
Ev'rything's right.
Oh, what a night
 for love.

A lavender breeze,
Summer perfume,
Sycamore trees,
Roses in bloom
Ev'rything's right;
Oh, what a night
 for love.

 The air is cool, but warm
 Are your lips,
 Warm is the touch
 Of your fingertips,

Some marshmallow clouds,
Silver lagoon,
Somewhere a sweet
Lullaby tune;
Ev'rything's right,
Oh, what a night
 for love.

Everybody Seems to Know I Love You

"Everybody Seems to Know I Love You" is just one more way of conveying that old conventional message, except that the singer is complaining that his beloved apparently isn't quite getting the message.

Everybody seems to know I love you;
Anyone could tell how much I care.
You're the only one who doesn't know it,
Doesn't seem to sense what's in the air.

Can't you see the way I'm always smiling
Just because you walk into my sight?
Haven't you at least begun to wonder
Why you turn my darkness into light?

This is my confession that you're hearing;
I can't keep the secret any more.
I expect to hear the people cheering
Now they know for sure who I adore.

You're the answer to my ev'ry prayer, love.
Now's the time to enter paradise.
That's what we'll be doing if we share love.
Does it really come as a surprise?

Nicotine and Caffeine and Cathleen

A country-western novelty with touches of wry humor. This song refers to the addictive power of love or physical attraction. The melody was provided by Richard Mears.

I suffer from three addictions
And they're really kinda bad afflictions,
So I'll never get very far
But let me tell you just what they are.
Nicotine–and caffeine–and Cathleen.

Nicotine–and caffeine–and Cathleen
What a scene!
Nicotine–and caffeine–and Cathleen;
You know what I mean?

Oh. I'm all hung up; it ain't no joke
I gotta have a smoke
And a cuppa jamoke.
Nicotine–and caffeine–and Cathleen

The woman ain't doin' me any good;
Everybody warned me in the neighborhood
But the shady lady said she's misunderstood
Cathleen–I should'a fled the scene
Nicotine–and caffeine–and Cathleen.

You Might as Well Give Up

The mood of this song-poem is playful, partly because of its boastfulness. The speaker, apparently practiced at bending others to his will, suggests to his companion that no further time need be wasted in delaying her surrender.

All's fair in love and war they say,
so here is my communique;

I'm overcoming your defenses.
My friend, it's clear
The end is near.

You might as well give up,
Got you surrounded.
You'll never get away.

You might as well surrender,
Just as a town did
In Julius Caesar's day.

I've got a plan
To capture you,
Enrapture you
      my dear.

And I'm the man
Who'll *see* it through
If it takes all year.

You might as well come out
With both your hands up;
My love, you met defeat.

As for my propaganda
It really stands up
So, baby, I repeat

This just might be
Your one last chance.
Open your arms;
Accept romance.

My terms are tender
If you surrender
      now.

Saturday Evening Post

In my youth the Post *was a true American institution. Its covers alone, many of which were done by Norman Rockwell, were charming and the contents were warmly typical of the time when American dreams were simpler and more civilized than at present. The melody is structured in a sort of Vaudeville, soft-shoe style.*

Saturday Evening Post.
Oh, how I used to love the
Saturday Evening Post.
Of all the magazines I read it
the very most.

I loved the pictures on the cover
And listen, lover,
Norman Rockwell drew those wonderful scenes–
of real Americana,
And Clarence Buddington Kelland used to
Write the funniest stories that you ever read.

It was really a kind of honor–
When the Saturday Evening Post
Was on your coffee-table
Everyone used to boast,
About the way they got the Saturday Evening Post.
Remember laughing at the old cartoons?
Talk about your Underground press, why say, boy
You can have your *Ramparts* and your *Playboy*

To the long lost days let's drink a toast–
Whatever happened to the Saturday Evening Post?

Ain't No Bad Time

The lyric is deliberately ungrammatical and rendered in lower middle-class street language. Its meaning is simply that when it comes to demonstrations of love and affection the timing seems always right.

I love to love you in the morning.
I love to love you in the night.
Ain't no bad time,
Baby, ain't no bad time.

I love to love you when it's rainin'
I love to love you in the sun.
Ain't no bad time,
Baby, ain't no bad time.

When something is great,
Whether early or late,
You can never ever get enough.
When there's somethin' so fine
As this love of mine,
Well, you know it's all
good stuff.

I love to love you in the summer.
I love to love you in the fall.
Ain't no bad time,

There's ev'ry reason and rhyme,
But there ain't no bad time
at all.

Millions and Millions of People

Film actress Janis Paige was the widow of the original publisher of a number of songs that had already been successful in Latin America. Of the several numbers she brought to my attention, for all of which I provided English-language lyrics, the one I liked best was a catchy samba by Walter Wonderly, the organist. I can't recall what the original title was but I chose to use the melody's structure as something of a sermon or commentary on our disorganized times.

Millions and millions of people are looking for thrills,
Millions and millions of people are looking for kicks.
They don't seem to notice the flowers
And they don't seem to notice the moonlight.

Isn't it sad
That they never
Look to the stars?

Millions and millions of people are looking for joy;
Flying and trying and buying some trivial toy.
Now why don't they listen to bluebirds?
And why don't they smile at the children?

Isn't it sad
That they never
Talk to the trees?

If they only had a brain
They'd see the sea.
If they listened to the rain
They would agree
with me.

Millions and millions of people are lonely and blue,
Crying and dying for something to give themselves to.
They don't seem to see all about them
Just how brightly the light shines above,
But millions and millions of people are looking for love.

Never Again

Everyone who has ever suffered from the breakup of a once satisfying love relationship is familiar with the fact that sadness can take a variety of forms. One of the most depressing is the realization, separate from the original cause of pain, that not only is the lover gone and lamented but there is now no possibility of his or her return.

Never again those arms,
Never again that funny face,
Never again those lips,
That set me aflame.

I find it hard to believe you're really gone;
In dreams I search for you until the dawn.
Never again those eyes,
Never again that sunny smile,

Never again those nights
We flew to the stars.
Friends say I'll love once more, but where?
But when?
My heart replies "Never again."

What Ever Happened to Romance?

This title, and lyric, occurred to me originally simply as a thought, with no necessary connection to music. I am of course hardly the first to observe the many depressing differences between life and professional entertainment of the glamourous period of the 1920s, '30s and '40s, and what passes for culture at present when glamour, good manners, and gentility seem to be little valued.

There was a time
When lovers thought about the moon.

There was a time
when lovers had their favorite tune.

There was a time
When poetry was all the rage.

And harbor lights,
And starry nights,
But that was quite a different age.

What ever happened to romance?
When love could thrill you with a gentle touch.
When just a knowing smile could mean so much,
What ever happened to romance?

What ever happened to the Spring?
When dreamers sang of April's tender rain,
Young hearts in love discovered lover's lane;
How can we bring it back again?

Times have changed
And it's not for the better.
Something's missing
along the way.

Once we knew
All the rules
To the letter.

Now we hardly
Know what to say.

What ever lies beyond today?
Can we recall the thrill
Of one shy glance,
The first sweet time a heart
Will take a chance?

What ever happened
How did it happen....
What ever happened to romance?

Happy Birthday, My Love

The melody of this number, which is deliberately evocative of the classic "Happy Birthday," expresses warm emotions connected with the beloved marking another of age's milestones.

Happy birthday, my love
Happy birthday, little girl grown tall,
And a kiss for every candle
    on your cake.

May your birthday wish come true,
May the fates be kind to you
And whatever I can do
    you can count on.

Happy birthday, my love
You have friends who care about you
Who would hate to do without you,
    so you see

We love you through the laughter
And the tears that may come after,
And a special happy birthday, love,
    from me.

We Might Have Been Wonderful

Oddly enough I had never realized, until the preparation of this manuscript, how many songs I have written, over the years, about failed love relationships. In this case the lover is speaking of an experience which was ended before it had come to full flower.

We probably would have fought a lot
From the very first.
You probably would have bought a lot
I'd consider the worst.

You probably would have cried
At the slightest provocation.
I probably would have died
At our first separation.

> But, oh–
> It might have been wonderful;
> And if it was wonderful,
> It might have been forever.
>
> You–
> Might have been oh, so warm,
> Safe harbor from any storm.
> It might have been forever.
>
> Who–
> Can predict what we might have achieved?
> You–
> Might have found it so hard to believe.

For we–
Might have been wonderful,
And if we were wonderful,
It would have been quite a show.
But now–
We'll never know.

There's a Girl in My Dreams

This song, recorded by vocalist Murray Ross, reminds us of the unfortunate complexity of love which, while it is undoubtedly one of the great blessings of life, nevertheless has confusing and negative power as well, depending on the breaks of the game. In this instance the speaker obviously takes his vows of loyalty seriously but is troubled by certain dream-visions.

When the day is over
And we go to sleep
Then the land of dreams awaits us all.

There are very sweet dreams,
And some incomplete dreams.
There are dreams we never quite recall.

But lately there's a certain face that haunts me,
A voice that softly speaks to me, yet taunts me.

But now some sweet mysterious perfume,
Some gentle smile, some warm and loving hand
Brings me close to paradise, then wakes me
Before I enter that enchanted land.

CHORUS:
There's a girl in my dreams
And it's not the right one.
There's a girl in my dreams
And it's making me sad.

I haven't strayed,
I haven't played,
And I don't plan to:
But there's a girl in my dreams
And she's driving me mad.

There's a face in my dreams
And it looks familiar.
There's a girl in my dreams
I seem to know.
I haven't lied,
I've not denied

The vows I'm bound by,
But there's a girl in my dreams
And she's bringing me low.

There's a voice in my dreams
And it seems to call me.
There's a smile in my dreams
And it thrills me through,
I know so well
She casts a spell
So swell and gentle,
But there's a nightmare ahead;
What can I do?
What can I do?
What can I do?

Golden Gate

A song of good strong quality is "I Left My Heart in San Francisco," made famous by the classic Tony Bennett recording, but it has always seemed to me that there was room for another number about the great foggy city. In this case, rather than compete with the earlier classic, I decided to write not about the community itself but about the world famous Golden Gate bridge. The lyric is more poetic than most.

VERSE:
There's a song about the man
Who left his heart in San Francisco.
There's a song about the city by the bay.
    They're pretty melodies
    But Mr. Leader, please
Play the song that puts my heart away.

CHORUS:
Golden Gate—I love you in the morning.
Golden Gate—you're beautiful by night.
That bridge that carries half-a-million little cars
Seems to lift my lonely heart up to the stars.

Golden Gate—you're beautiful in Springtime
    But lovely, too
    When driving through
    In Fall
I love London, Paris, Rome
But you bring my heart back home,

You old
Wonderful Gold–
    en Gate.

Lazy, lacy clouds
Floating in the sun,
High above the bay
When the day
    is done.

Lovers all remember
Strolling hand-in-hand.
It's so close to heaven,
That enchanted land.

Golden Gate–you warm my heart in Winter
And the sight of you is worth the longest wait.
No matter where I roam
You call my heart back home
You old
Wonderful Gold–
en Gate.

The Girl Can't Help It

This is a light, swinging, jazz-oriented song for which the lyric is expressed in a playfully boastful Sinatra-like tone.

The girl can't help it,
She's just naturally great.
The girl can't help it,
So when you go on a date,

All the people on the street
They just stop and stare.
They never saw anything quite so sweet,
Just standing there.

She really doesn't mean it,
She simply knocks you out.
And once they've seen it
Other women just stand and pout.

She's a beaut, she's so cute
And to boot
So fine.
And by the way, did I forget to say
She's mine!

Don't Cry, Little Girl

Although I have more-or-less an equal fondness for all my brain-children, this song is one of my favorites. Its message can be construed as directed either at an actual little girl — a child — or simply a young woman who has a certain sweetness and girlishness about her. Harmonically the melody is interesting because it starts in one key and ends in another.

Don't cry, little girl;
Just remember that you're my little girl,
And I'll try, little girl,
To keep you happy.

When you're caught in a storm
And the winds are blowing colder,
Well, you'll be cozy and warm
With your head on my shoulder.

Don't cry, little girl.
You'll remember how to fly, little girl,
And I'll dry all your tears
As we head for the years
to come.

You know, honey,
That it's funny
How we laughed all yesterday.
So don't cry, little girl—
Just come on out to play.

Let's Do It Again

It is typical of all of us, literally from infancy, that when we have had a pleasurable experience, of almost any sort, we quickly set about recreating it.

Remember that kiss?
Was it the kind of kiss you're startin' to miss?
May I remind you how we did it, and then—
Let's do it again.

Remember that thrill?
I love it, and I know that I always will,
So you can say when,
But let's do it again—and again.

I've been all around the track—once or twice
But it was so incredibly nice
And new, with you.
What am I gonna do with you
The rest of my life?

Remember that night,
The night we danced until the dawn's early light?
Well, let's repeat it all, my baby, and then
Let's do it again.
Let's do it,
Let's do it again.

Something Mysterious

This deliberately unusual song has been recorded by the brilliant arranger Tom Kubis and, with vocal, by Murray Ross. The lyric addresses an aspect of love that is rarely commented upon, that is its essentially mysterious nature. But the singer conveys a deeper and wider message, which is that life itself — including the very universe — is literally founded on mystery, given that we do not completely understand the factors of either time or space or — Einstein's concern — their inter-relationship.

There's something mysterious about this world,
There's something mysterious in time.
There's something mysterious about space
And there's something mysterious–in your face.

There's something so mystical about this life
There's a wonder in the thunder of your heart.
There's something mysterious in truth and lies,
And there's something mysterious–in your eyes.

We don't know the beginning
And we'll never, ever know the end.
We're losing even when we're winning
So accept it, old friend.

There's something mysterious in silence.
There's something that's magical in sound.
There's something mysterious when you're coming home,
Even more when you're outward bound.

The House at Malibu

This song, very nicely recorded by Ginger Berglund, is in ideal terms a one-chorus story because of its surprise ending.

They have a house–at Malibu
But they are hardly ever there together.
The seas are blue
At Malibu
    but so are they.

There was a time–when love was sweet
And everything seemed possible and true,
Another town,
A simpler life,
And oh, so many happy things to do

    But then–shadows darkened ev'ry sunrise,
    Ah, then, every blessing had a cost.
    One dream–they never could recapture
    And so their paradise–was lost.

So there's the house–at Malibu,
So beautiful it almost makes you cry.
No doubt you've guessed
Who's living there;
The tragic pair–
My love and I.

That-a-Girl

This common statement of encouragement is addressed to a young woman who has already been knocked about a bit by life, as we all are in time, and who therefore stands in need of some cheering up.

That-a-Girl
Keep your little chin up!
That-a-girl
You can be strong.

When things go wrong
Don't let it get you down
Have a little heart-break,
Frown a little frown.

And you will learn
Why ev'ry spring
Each lonely blue-bird
Relearns how to sing.

That-a-girl,
Looking for the rainbow,
That-a-girl,
Flashing that grin.

Never give in
You've much too much to lose
Never mind the storm clouds,
You can take the blues.

There'll be a someone,
Just wait and see.
Almost any day now...
he could come your way now.

Ev'ry one will say now
That-a-girl
That-a-girl

Could You Be the One?

This song existed as a melody for several weeks before I was able to find a title and approach with which I was satisfied. It refers to the very early stage of a man/woman relationship in which the speaker begins to get glimmerings about the possible importance of the attraction he feels and yet is far from certain of the outcome.

Stranger, could you be the one?
Could you be the one,
For me?

Tell me—could this be the day
I will find my way,
To all that's lovely?

Dreams—sometimes do come true.
Are there dreams,
That two can feel?

Could our hearts demand
That the things we planned,
Be real?

Dreamer, could this be the time
Life becomes sublime
for us?

Baby, could you be my one and only love?
If we waited so long
Would it be wrong
Or should we just dive in?

Stranger, if you're game
Let the games begin.

Sunday in Town

This is a very New York song, although it could be construed as applying to any large city in the world — Chicago, London, Paris or any other. Urban residents, for understandable reasons, are in the habit of getting out of town on weekends, if their circumstances permit, but in this case the lover decides that he doesn't really need mountain greenery or seacoast air; it might be better to remain in town and simply devote all his time to the woman he loves.

Friday
Is often my day
To head for the hills,
Cure all my ills
　　in the country.

Friday
Is often my day
For calling it quits
Here in the pits
　　of this town.

But this time, my love,
Why don't we turn it down?

CHORUS:
Sunday in town,
The park looks so inviting today.
Sun shinin' down
And there's the sound of children at play.
Down on your knees
To give thanks for that breeze
That's hereabout.
Hip, hip hooray,
It's the kind of a day
To cheer about.

Sleepy old town,
It's like a desert island for two.
Sunday in town's
A honeymoon vacation with you.

(continued)

Summer is ready to leave us.
The leaves turning golden and brown.
Lets this girl and boy
    enjoy
Another Sunday in town.

My Wild Imagination

I write so much music — having reached the 8,000th song level in August of 1999 — that I have hazy recollections, at best, as to precisely when and where I wrote most of my numbers. In this case, however, I do recall that the melody occurred to me when I was idly fingering the piano keys backstage in a theater in Denver, when Jayne and I were on a national tour of Noel Coward's delightful Tonight at 8:30. *I did not sit down at the piano with the intention of writing a song. It was simply my habit each evening to relax by doing a bit of playing before the curtains went up, not particularly caring whether or not people in the audience could hear what I was doing. Suddenly, without my having intended it, I realized that I had played quite a pretty passage. I went back to the top of it again and the rest of the number was completed in literally less than a minute. The lyric was added some months later and speaks of that sort of turmoil of thought that is characteristic of the experience of being in love. The lover, in this case, obviously feels insecure but does permit himself to fantasize about some very pleasant possibilities.*

My wild imagination
Makes me feel
You some day may make all my day-dreams real.

The craziest idea
I think of when you're near
But still, my love, I fear
　　I can't reveal.

My wild imagination
Sometimes seems
To take its inspiration from my dreams,
For then I can imagine that you love me, too.
Imagine what will happen when you do.

My wild imagination seems to say
Though love was lost I'll love another day
Perhaps 'cause I'm a dope
I entertain the hope
Your loving arms will open,
　　Come what may

(continued)

My wild imagination sometimes sings
Of wishing wells, hotels, and wedding rings.
Imagine, if you can, one honeymoon for two.
Imagine my excitement when you do
And all my wild imaginings come true.

Francesca

Whenever a composer or lyricist writes a song with a woman's name there is inevitably conjectures as to whether it is autobiographical. In this case the title came from the name of one of the two main characters in the popular novel The Bridges of Madison County. *Although I assumed he had already made other plans for a title theme and musical score I nevertheless sent a copy of it, with a brief note, to Clint Eastwood before the film was made.*

Francesca, you're with me now.
Francesca, I don't know how,
But when there's moonlight
It brings me you, Francesca.

I love you, and always will;
You're with me, at least until
The end of time comes.
My heart is yours, Francesca.

Night and day, you're part of everything I long for
Day and night, you're in my every dream.
Wrong or right, you're what I sing my lonely song for.
Can you hear my heart's romantic theme?

Francesca, though we're apart,
Francesca, you're in my heart.
I pray, dear, someday we'll meet again
I'll wait dear,
Until that where and when.

I Don't Know If You're the Love of My Life

(***Rock ballad***)

In this instance the speaker, obviously in the early phase of a love relationship, has little or no idea as to whether the emotions he presently feels will long persist. Nevertheless he simply give himself to them on a carefree, come-what-may basis.

I don't know if you're
The love of my life,
That will take some time
To figure out.

Will I know for sure
The love of my life,
Or will I forever
Be in doubt?

But in the meantime,
You're just what I need.
I like what you say,
I like what you read.

Something about you
Is terribly sweet.
The touch of your hand
Can make me feel grand.

Will you prove to be
The love of my life?
Only time will tell,
They say.

And if we're headed
For a nasty spill,
You're still
The love of my life
today.

I Do Not Think of You

So far as I know this particular aspect of the tragedy of a lost or absent love has never before been commented upon. Sometimes in the heat of such emotions lovers overstate the case and claim that they think of the absent one constantly. This, of course, is not possible, strictly speaking.

I do not think of you every minute
Or even ev'ry hour,
To tell the truth,
But there are never any days
I do not think of you.

Upon awak'ning
I desire you,
At certain music
I desire you,
And at the sight of certain places and reminders
I am reminded, my love.

When I hear thunder
Ah, then I wonder
Where you are.
When I see lightning
It can be fright'ning
When you're far.

The scent of flowers
Recalls the hours
You were here.
The glow of moonlight
Recalls the June night
You were near–
My dear.

When I hear singing
My thoughts go winging
Back to you.
When I hear laughter
Forever after
You'll come through.

(continued)

I do not think of you
All throughout the day,
But there are never any days
I do not think of you.

I Can See It All Now

This number, which I believe was written in the late 1950s, is one in which the lover permits his imagination to roam as he entertains glamourous and appealing scenes involving himself and his beloved. The lyric closes, however, with a surprise ending, expressing the speaker's insecurities.

I can see it all now,
You with that breakfast laughter,
You on the morning after
with me,

I can see it all now,
You with those blue pajamas
Down in the warm Bahamas
with me.

Imagination is a wonderful thing;
It makes me hear
So loud and clear,
Those wedding bells ring.

I can see it all now,
You with those toothpaste kisses.
Darling, it's clear that this is
my plan.

I can see it all now;
Am I the only one
who can?

If I Only Had the Chance

The message of this lyric is particularly wistful given that something—never explained—is keeping the lovers apart. So the singer contents himself with thinking of the many ways in which he will be of the most loving service to his beloved, if only fate will provide the opportunity.

I would bake you pies,
I would bring you tea.
I would buy you silly gifts like fancy pants.
I would love to do
A million tender things,
If I only had the chance.

I would say your prayers,
Cover you at night,
Tell you ancient stories of divine romance.
I would daily do
A million lovely things,
if I only had the chance.

Sing songs for you,
Right wrongs for you,
And I'm the Cinderella (woman's lyric)
To carry your umbrella

I could dry your tears,
I would lock your door,
I would gladly water all your indoor plants,
All your life I'd do
A million tender things,
If I only had the chance,
If I only had the chance.

II

I would bring you juice,
Flowers on your tray,
Bring you funny shoes, my dear, to make you dance.
I would take such care
Of you, my only love,
If I only had the chance.

I would bring you joy,
I would bring you toys,
And on Christmas, give you holly-berry plants.
I would do so many lovely things for you
If I only had the chance.

At break of day
Kiss dreams away,
And then at night, my dear,
I'd bring a light, for cheer.

I would give you books,
I would bring you wine
And in cozy nooks, my dear
we would recline.
And when you were lonely,
Bring you sweet romance.
Oh, so many things I'd do
If I only had the chance.

Goodbye, Mr. Evans

When I heard this song's remarkably beautiful and harmonically rich melody, by musician Phil Woods, I immediately felt that it should have a lyric. Phil agreed. Given that his melody was written in respectful memory of the great and influential pianist Bill Evans, I decided to draw out the original message in lyric form. Evans was by no means just another gifted jazz player. He was something quite special and had a uniquely creative way with harmony which perhaps only other professional musicians can fully appreciate. Bill was also personally a tragic figure who died too young, a victim of drug addiction, a tragedy against which his own high intelligence did not protect him.

I

There was once a man
And his name was Bill
And we miss him now
And we always will.

He discovered lights
That some eyes can't see,
Somehow made us learn to hear
A secret harmony.

There were magic sounds
And so many times,
When he touched the keys;
We heard angel-chimes.

And in years ahead
When the angels strum
On their magic harps
Happy tears may come.

When we stop to think
Who our heroes are
We should be ashamed
Such a blazing star

Lived among us once
And so few were hip
That his heart was launched
On a lonely trip

II

Oh, if only time
Could rewind the years
And our foolish hearts
Could recall the tears,

But the man is gone
Though his songs remain.
Treasure every note
To relieve the pain.

Goodbye Mr. E.
(echo) Mystery.

Barbecued Ribs

This boogie-woogie style song was written in the late 1940s, when I was quite new at the trade. It describes an imaginary rib joint in San Francisco, frequented by the late-night crowd.

Way up in San Francisco, there's a joint call'd Joe's.
Shortly after midnight when they close the shows,
The cats all gather. Because they'd rather.
Roll up their sleeves, 'n put on their bibs,
And have a mess of barbecued ribs.

Now there's a little trio on a tiny stage,
They play the latest music and they're all the rage,
But what you eat there. That is the treat there.
Because Joe is a kick; you should see his nibs,
Serve a mess of barbecued ribs.

Oh they're crisp, and brown,
They're the best, in town.
You can pick 'em right up and eat 'em with your fingers,
When the ribs are gone, the taste still lingers.

If ever you're in Frisco and you pass the spot,
You look in through the window and the fire is hot,
Well brother then you, call for a menu.
Prepare for a treat, I ain't tell-in' fibs,
You'll blow your top on barbecued ribs.

A Clown Standing in the Rain

As regards this number, the melody came first, the lyric was added several weeks thereafter. Because the melody is strongly emotional I wanted to devise a lyric that had the same quality.

The show has just left town
But here's a clown
Standing in the rain;
And everybody laughs to see him,
Mindless of his pain.

The songs, the games, the fun,
They all are done,
Gone forevermore.
Still we see the lonely figure,
Standing at the door.

A girl there was,
Lovelier than spring
As she floated through the air
High above the ring.

The man—who stands apart
Has lost his heart,
Helpless to explain
How passers-by can smile to see him
Standing in the rain.

I Talk to You Every Day

This song, which has been tastefully recorded by Ginger Berglund, refers to the habit, familiar to all those who have been in love, of literally speaking to the absent beloved, whether aloud or not.

I talk to you—every day.
You can't hear me,
You're not here,
But I talk to you every day,
And somehow it helps, my dear.

I call to you—every night
In the shadows of my dreams.
Can you feel the blazing light
As I call to you?

Just to hear your name aloud
When I'm lonely in a crowd
Makes my heart forget its fears.
And a lovely melody
That we sometimes sang off-key
makes me smile, despite my tears.

I talk to you—all the time
When I'm working
Or alone,

In a neighborhood cafe,
That I pass along the way,
I talk to you
every day.

Tell Me Your Dreams

This song was written "to order" when Hollywood publicist Warren Cowan, who was at the time assigned to handle public relations for a book titled Tell Me Your Dreams, *by the best-selling novelist Sidney Sheldon, thought his task might be facilitated if a song with the same title as the novel could be written. I agreed to provide the number.*

The storyline of the lyric, as it happens, has nothing to do with that of the book itself, which concerns an investigation into a series of murders.

I pointed out to Sidney and Warren that it wasn't necessary to refer to the original plot because there was already film and music-world precedent that showed a title alone, in either form, would automatically draw attention to the other form. The famous ballads "Gone with the Wind," "I Cover the Waterfront" and "Laura" were other examples.

At dawn—alone by the sea,
You wakened to me
And told me you'd been dreaming.

Then—alone on the sand,
My heart in your hand,
You told me that you loved me,

But now you're gone
And summer has flown away;
Gone—the lovely dream we shared.

So now—recalling your eyes,
I roam paradise,
But never can I find you.

Could you know
I long for you so?
Here on the shore, dear,
We once explored, dear
Could you once more, dear,
Tell me your dream?

We're Missing Mr. Porter

This lyric, which is about the great Cole Porter, a gifted composer and lyricist, is, of course, about more than the man himself. It's about the loss of glamour and sophistication — among other once valued qualities — in our present vulgar and classless age. As Gene Lees observed in his introduction to this work, there have never been many songwriters who provided both lyrics and music. And even among those so competent they are often far better at one branch of the art than the other. Steven Sondheim, for example, is an absolutely brilliant lyricist, perhaps — depending on the criteria — the best ever, but no critic or peer has ever made the same high judgment of him as a composer. Johnny Mercer — as mentioned above, my favorite lyricist — also wrote a few top-grade melodies of which Dream *and* Jamboree Jones *are two of my favorites, but his reputation rests almost entirely on his original and sensitive song-poems. Cole Porter, by way of contrast, was equally adept at the keyboard and the notepad.*

We're missing Mr. Porter.
He could make us dream so.
What an elegant guy.
Was he born in black tie?
It seems so.

That sophistication,
Where did it go?
We've replaced the romantic
With the frantic,
The high with the low.

He helped us handle heartbreak,
Showed how to love once more.
With what delicate knife
He sculpted the life
On the 90th floor.

Let us now praise famous men
We'll not see soon again,
So here's to Mr. Porter.
Three cheers to Mr. Porter.
Raise a glass to Mr. Porter,
To the class of Mr. Porter,
In that great mysterious where or when.

There She (He) Goes

This, too, is one of my oldest songs, having been written in 1947. It was originally recorded, shortly after being created, by Tommy Mara then done again by the gifted Irene Kral in an album of my material that she recorded for the United Artists label. It concerns the sad spectacle of the lover standing transfixed as his now lost love comes into view and walks past.

There she goes;
I guess I'll pretend not to see,
There she goes,
I wonder if she noticed me;
Gee, it's funny
After all the pain
How the feeling never seems to wane.

Someone new
Is walking beside her tonight,
Someone who
Had better be treating her right;

Though she couldn't care as much as I
Cross my heart and really hope to die.
She's looking rather well,
But you can never tell,

I wonder if she ever thinks of me;
If they should come my way,
I wonder what I'd say,
And now my tears
Have made it rather hard to see.

I suppose—my heart should be looking around,
But it knows love's easier lost than it's found;
Can't forget her—
And I guess it shows,
There's the one I love and—there she goes.

Mr. New York

It is not simply the fact that this number's title refers to New York City that makes it what I call a New York song. It would be quite a simple matter, after all, to write a song in the country style, with the speaker literally situated in Oklahoma, and yet providing us with his comments on the great Eastern metropolis. What gives this song its identifiable ambiance is that it describes a character who is very much part of the social lore of Manhattan in the glamourous days in which Cole Porter contributed so much to the city's cultural reputation. What passes for Cafe Society at present is strikingly different from that of a world that was defined by the Broadway Theater, The Stork Club, Walter Winchell's column, and the popular song lyrics of not only the inimitable Cole but also Lorenz Hart, Ira Gershwin, Howard Deitz and Oscar Hammerstein.

Hollywood, too, contributed its own impression of New York's reality and gave us leading ladies who were glamourous and feminine, and leading men attired in white tie and tails.

Shakespeare can hardly have been literally the first to observe that beauty is in the eye of the beholder, but the same is even more true of glamour, which is always a combination of reality and now professionally-induced illusion. But what a sweet illusion that of the Cole Porter period was as compared with the sadistic ugliness which is commercially marketed at present , apparently for the appallingly tragic reason that there is an audience that thrives on it.

Mr. New York
That's what you were;
Out every night on the town
Looking for her,

There was nothing it seemed
That you didn't own.
But we didn't know
That after the show
You were so alone.

Mr. New York;
Prince of the city,
Picking up checks
As you looked for your ex
Around town.

The love of your life
Has drifted away,
So what does it mean
To be Mr. New York today?

I Dream Again

Humans — both as individuals and as a race — seem literally unable to long survive in the total absence of hope. There is, of course, an endless series of separate questions as to specifically what is hoped for, but in those fortunately rare situations in which there is no possibility of rescue or relief from suffering, the most rational solution may be to surrender to fate, to give up. But because this is a depressing perception we do like to be reminded that in most even troublesome situations, there is usually some reason to hope and plan for a better future. The following lyric has a purposeful naiveté.

When a dream goes wrong
I dream again,
Sing a happy song
And dream again,
'Cause there's always tomorrow
And time to dream again.

When my plans fall through
I realize
That each day is new
With fresh surprise
So I don't give up
Oh, no, I dream again,

Sometimes a cloudy day
Can make me feel so gloomy
But that's the very way
April brings the flowers to me.

When the things I've done
All fall apart
Then I just repair
My broken heart
For there's always tomorrow
And time to dream again.

Funny Lady

When I perform comedy concerts, which I'm constantly doing in all parts of the country, I almost invariably work with a pianist named Paul Smith, who is prodigiously gifted. For a good many years he was Ella Fitzgerald's personal accompanist and has worked with major artists and orchestra leaders for most of his life. Lest it seem odd that a pianist should require the services of another player of the same instrument, I'll explain that Paul is engaged chiefly to play during my vocals since, for reasons unknown to me, I don't particularly enjoy playing and singing at the same time. Smith is famous, within the music industry, for his incredible dexterity at the keyboard, a gift which calls to mind that mastery of the instrument we associate with Art Tatum or Oscar Peterson. It is not as well known that he's also a highly competent composer. When I joined him, not long ago, at a technical run-through, the purpose of which is to check microphones, loudspeakers, lighting and staging equipment, I heard him idly playing a lovely melody. On the assumption that any song that well-written would already have come to my attention if it had been introduced into the popular library, I thought at once that it might be an original melody of Paul's creation, which turned out to be the case. Moreover he had already given it a title so I didn't have to conceive one in writing the following lyric.

Funny lady—so they say
But I saw you—cry today.
You didn't think that anyone was near
But I was there, and now it's very clear
Funny lady, from the start
You disguised a broken heart.

Somehow you always make us laugh
But those out front don't know the half.
I salute you for the courage you display
Funny lady—keep us smiling every day.

What Will I Do When We Meet Again?

For God knows what evolutionary purpose, the majority of even sincere love relationships do not persist. And even when a pair of participants have resigned themselves to the closing of such a chapter of their lives they are often troubled by the question as to how they might conduct themselves if, at some future point, they happened to meet again. In the following lyric the speaker has obviously not reached the point of total resignation and is therefore fearful that he might reveal his emotions in the event of such a meeting.

What will I do
When next we meet?
How will I act
If you try to attract
    my attention?

Will I be nonchalant
And deny you're the thing I want?
Or will I look somewhere above you
And pretend that I don't love you?

What will I say
If we meet by chance?
Will I seem very grave myself,
As I try to behave myself?

How can I possibly prepare
To pretend that I don't care?
Love of my life, if you come into view
Please tell me, what will I do?

Junior Prom

Once the record company had decided to have a contract artist do this number, Joni James was a good choice in that part of her popular appeal was based on her basic natural sound which was that of a teenager, very feminine and girlish.

If I had written the lyric first, or even thought merely of the title, the melody probably would not have been a waltz because as of the 1950s there were not many actual waltzes played at high school proms, whether senior or junior. But since the melody was already a given I chose to deal with the problem by simply ignoring it. One working with such sweet, simple storylines must guard against the kind of lyric sophistication characteristic of the writing of, say, Cole Porter or Steven Sondheim. Irvin Berlin's lyric style would be a more reasonable model. I permitted myself, nevertheless, one brief touch of cleverness near the end of the number:

Dad will be mad
If he finds that I'm gad-
ding with every Dick, Harry, and Tom—

Waltz me around, with my feet
Off the ground,
At the Junior Prom.
While we're swaying,
The orchestra's playing
Our song.

Hold me politely,
But ever so tightly,
While lights are low,
I can't recall a more wonderful
Promenade Ball.
Moments so sweet,
We can never repeat
At a Junior Prom.

And while we dance,
We may find there's romance
In the air.

(continued)

Dad will be mad, if he finds
That I'm gadding with ev'ry
Dick, Harry or Tom;
But gee!
It's a wonderful world at the
Junior Prom.

On the Beach

Given that a fine melody was written by Ernest Gold for the film On the Beach, *starring Ava Gardner and Fred Astaire, anyone providing a lyric obviously had to start from that point. The actual storyline of the motion picture dealt with the ever-present dangers of nuclear holocaust but given the singable nature of the melody a lyric on that subject matter would have been inappropriate. I therefore took the same general direction that had earlier worked well in the case of the film* Picnic *and described a romantic encounter in which the beauties of nature were part of the incident's overall loveliness.*

You were walking on the beach
On that lovely summer's day,
Oh, so very near and yet far away.

Ev'ry ocean breeze
That played about you,
Seemed like symphonies
That sang of love.

You were walking
On the beach
On that lovely summer's day,

Oh, so very near and yet
Far away.
Ev'ry ocean breeze

That played about you,
Seemed like symphonies
That sang of love.

You were walking on the beach
And the sun was in your hair
And I saw you standing there
Out of reach.

Then you smiled my way,
My heart went winging,
As you seemed to say,
"Will this be love?"

(continued)

That's the day my life began,
In that moment dreams came true,
When I fell in love with you
On the beach.

Wheelchairs, Crutches and Canes

A couple of years back when I was on a tour of a great many cities — working with my old comedy aides Louis Nye and Bill Dana, pianist Paul Smith and singer Marilyn May, I was stricken with one of the worst cases of sciatica known to — well, to me. If I had been working alone I would have considered myself entirely justified in calling off the scheduled appearances in the last several cities, but because I was part of a traveling troop and didn't want to put the others out of work I spent a good part of the next two years getting on various stages, airplanes, ships, etc., with the aid of either wheelchairs, crutches or canes.

Obviously a performer whose general good health has been self-evident for decades cannot suddenly appear on stage physically indisposed without dealing frankly with his problem, since the attention of audiences will be drawn to it as soon as he appears. I ended up dispensing with my usual sort of introductory material — rambling, as spontaneous as it is — and instead joked about my predicament. Example: "As you've noticed, I had a bit of difficulty getting out here but I don't want you to worry about it. It's just an old football injury." After the disbelieving laughter, since my professional image is hardly that of a former professional athlete, I said, "No, really. This morning, coming out of my garage, I tripped on an old football."

VERSE:
Some people drive–and some people fly,
They're more lucky by far, than I.
Some people run, or meander or sidle
But I sit here thinking thoughts suicidal.
Some are running or jogging on treadmill or track
While I'm–
Most of the time–
Flat on my back.

(continued)

CHORUS: (Waltz tempo)

Wheelchairs, crutches and canes,
That's how I'm getting about.
I'm crutching and caning
But I'm not complaining
Despite just a touch of the gout.

Be you milk-maid or Duchess
Sometimes you'll need crutches
'Cause that's just the breaks of the game.
But it's quite a surprise
When you first realize
Your excuses and you are both lame.

(EVERYBODY!)

Wheelchairs, crutches and canes,
Can a walker be next on my list?
As for dancing, forget it
Waterloo? I have met it.
And I'll never again keep a tryst.

Sure, it's tough when you've hobbled
On streets that are cobbled,
Or all such uneven terrain,
And you walk like a chimp
So they're calling you gimp;
It could easily drive you insane.

Stop Me Before I Shop Again

Song writer-producer Allan Jay Friedman had approached me about collaborating on a theatrical musical titled Working Girl's Guide to Romance, *the story of Kristy, a sweet, pretty and thankfully unsophisticated young woman from Iowa who had come to the big city and has assorted adventures — positive and negative — that are a part of such social transitions.*

One of the new friends she makes is her landlady who, in her capacity as a veteran New Yorker, offers to show Kristy the ropes. To make the older woman somewhat less theatrical and more real I decided to have her suffer from the curse of compulsive shopping, a weakness she willingly confesses to in the following lyric.

Stop me—before I shop again!
Stop me—'cause I'm getting that urge
To splurge.

Calling Marcus, calling Neiman,
And all able-bodied seamen.
No matter what I see I covet,
I need it—I love it.

I confess that, yes, I want it
And I've simply got to flaunt it.
I'll take it in or I'll enlarge it
Whether I pay cash of charge it.
So stop me—before I shop again!

If I see—there's a sale
Anywhere in the whole Blooming-dale,
If I see—they're lowering prices,
Right away I recall what my vice is.

If I see that the prices are slashed,
I recall where my money is stashed.
Only time when I'm really alive
Is when reeling through Beverly Drive—

Lady, tell the truth, haven't you
Gone insane—on 7th Avenue?
Somebody call a copper;
You've got to stop this shopper.
Yes, stop me—before I shop again!

(continued)

If I see those Sunday pages
My reaction is outrageous,
When I read the bargain sections,
I run off in all directions.

But self-control
I'm unequal to the task,
That's why I ask
Stop me, before I shop again!

When the madness strikes
And I first begin to feel it
And I know I'll either purchase it—or steal it,
I don't know where I'll be when I yield.
Though I'm partial to Marshall
And his field.
I know it sounds stupid and dumb,
But I've found
That I'm bound
To succumb.

Please contradict me. You must prevent me,
Otherwise I may tell them all you sent me.
Apprehend me,
Don't defend me.
You security guards, please surround me
I won't be hateful, merely grateful—
That you found me.

Now if the sale is referred to as a clearance,
Somehow it changes my appearance.
I'm degraded, demeaned
When I act like a fiend;
I can't control the amount
That I charge to my account
Yet there's a sadness
To this madness,
Even badness

I readily confess,
When they cut prices by half,
You may scoff, you may laugh,
But I've simply got to have that dress.
When they tell me it's "the latest"
Well, by me, that means the greatest.
Though the merchandise is shoddy,

I would gladly sell my body,
And my will is much too frail
To desist or resist a bargain sale.
So stop me
Go ahead and pop me
Stop me–before I shop again.

You're Just a White Man Singin' Like a Black Man

It has been commonly recognized since early in this century, even — I assume — by white racists, that the primary contribution to the field of jazz has come from the black community. Fortunately there has over the decades been no shortage of gifted white jazz artists but they themselves have always properly revered their black peers.

Oddly enough the same perception does not seem to have applied in the field of rock. I am conscious of having heard, in early childhood, black gospel music, big band swing and other rhythmic forms, largely black in origin, which flowed into the broad and deep stream that is rock.

Both key terms are, of course, extremely general in that each field itself is divided into a great number of separate forms and styles.

But if there's anything that distinguishes the constellation of styles employed by white rock singers it is that, unlike African-American vocalists, they rarely sing in their natural vocal communication style. If you meet the average white rock vocalist socially you will have little trouble understanding what he says, and indeed if you hadn't previously been told what he does for a living you might well never guess. To hurry to the point, the average white rocker sings in two dominant modes, both of which are in social reality utterly foreign to him. The most common is black, the other is rural.

In the case of white vocalists who are themselves from the American South — Elvis Presley and Jerry Lee Lewis, for example — their singing style is therefore authentic. But there are vocalists from Seattle, Chicago, Boston and numerous other northern cities who never spent a day in the South in their life and ordinarily communicate with no trace of either a rural or Southern accent, but who nevertheless adopt such personas when they sing.

Perhaps the first whites to sing like blacks were the minstrel entertainers of the 19th and early 20th centuries. Although young people today may construe this as a simple instance of racism's typical lack of respect, I don't believe this was the case, except in rare instances. Such esteemed white performers as Al Jolson, Eddie Canter and George M. Cohan worked in blackface and intended no disrespect in doing so.

Many whites were honestly amused by black speech and manners and indeed that is still the case. For that matter over the years many black entertainers have themselves "made fun" of the speech of rural or urban-poor blacks.

That at least is the background thought that led me to write the following lyric.

You're just a white man
Singin' like a black man
Ain't nothin' original
About you.

You're lookin' pretty sloppy
Both front and back, man,
And all you do is copy
Better singers than yourself.

You're just a white man
Singin' like a black man,
But you're a star
And the other guy's sittin' on the shelf.

There ain't no justice
At least not enough.
They could rock 'n roll it
And then somebody stole it
And that ain't right.

You're just a square man
Singin' like a hip man
You ain't nowhere, man
Jumpin' all around.

You're just a white man
Singin' like a black man
And you're not the one
Who pioneered that ground.

Cutie Pants

Composer/bassist Ray Brown was so pleased with the lyric I provided for his catchy jazz number "Gravy Waltz" that he asked me to do another, in this instance for an untitled melody based on a tricky little lick, again in the jazz-waltz category.

Because of its unusual structure, which consists of a good many short lines, the lyric naturally had to conform to the rhythm of the music.

In any event, the song lucked out in that the first person to record it was the great jazz artist Carmen McCrea.

I

Like the way you prance around,
Kinda fancy-pants around,
Let me see you dance around,
Cutie pants, my cutie pants.

Pretty little nose you've got,
Love the sassy clothes you've got,
And the these and those you've got,
Cutie pants, my cutie pants.

Why chug-a-lug?
Let's kiss and hug,
Snug as a bug
Dug in a rug.

Call me on the phone if you
Ever feel alone and blue.
I'll be there to comfort you,
Cutie pants, my cutie pants.

II

I'm the king if you're the queen,
Cutest thing I've ever seen,
Gotta tell you what I mean,
Cutie pants, my cutie pants.

There's a lot of talk around,
'Bout the way you walk around,
Draws a line a block around,
Cutie pants, my cutie pants.

That certain thing
Your kisses bring,
Just makes me sing
Ring-ding-a-ding.

Dig the groovy style of you,
Mona Lisa smile of you,
Don-cha know that I love you,
Cutie pants, my cutie pants.

What Kind of Fool?

Quite a few years before Anthony Newly and Leslie Bricuss's classic ballad "What Kind of Fool Am I?" I had written a number with a somewhat similar title. My version, by way of contrast, was more in the rhythmic, slow-jazz category in style reminiscent of the delightful lyrics that Johnny Burke used to provide for the melodies of one my favorite composers, Jimmy Van Heusen.

What kind of fool
Falls in love
Just because he sees a handful of stars
    in the sky?

What kind of dope
Falls in love
Just because the breeze is singin'
    A sweet lullaby?

And tell me, what kind of sap
Walks right into the trap
The yellow moon sets out?

Tells how it feels,
Falling head over heels,
For someone who
Just makes him blue?

What kind of fool gives his heart
Long before he knows there's
Any demand to supply?
I'll tell you what kind of fool
If you promise not to laugh
At a fool such as I.

Yes, I was the dope
Who was hopin'
You'd open
Your arms,
If I sang my song
What kind of fool could be
Oh, so wrong!

And Even Then

Although the fate of most love relationships does not always conform to the rosy predictions that lovers typically feel while in the early throes of a romantic attachment, such emotions are nevertheless entirely legitimate. The farthest stretch to which the imagination of the lover can take him or her is to the point of either the end of his own life or of time itself.

Until the flowers bloom without the rain,
And there's no moon above the purple plain;
Till there's no sense of where or when—
My love is yours—and even then.

Until the brightest star has left the sky,
Until the end of time is drawing nigh;
And poets will not lift the pen—
My love is yours—and even then.

And though these words I'm employing—
So incompletely convey
All of the fire in my desire,
Still I'll go on and say:

Till there's no power in the stormy sea,
Until our day is part of history;
Until we know what might have been—
My love is yours—and even then.

It's Gehockta Leber Day

To the eternal question put to all the world's composers and lyricists, "Where do you get the ideas for your songs?" there is, of course, an infinity of answers. As regards the next number, its genesis came from a chance meeting with my friend comedian Buddy Hackett at a show-biz dinner some months ago. After a meandering conversation about the usual cabbages and kings, Buddy said, "By the way, there's a class for beginners in Yiddish that's starting at the University of Judaism and I'm gonna sign up for it. Do you want to go with me?"

On the spur of the moment I said, "Sure."

There's no bias in the fact that I probably would not have so readily agreed if Buddy had been talking about Swedish, Swahili or Gaelic, given that one rarely encounters them in the context of the entertainment professions, whereas Yiddish is often heard. In any event I did indeed sign up for the course, which was taught by a charming woman named Marion Herbst. I reported for instruction Tuesday nights at six o'clock for the following several weeks, though I missed a few classes because I was performing on those evenings. The punch line to the story is that Buddy never showed up, although when I met him at another social event and kidded him about his absence he did join me on the last session of the course.

Someone asked me, early on, why I was studying Yiddish, to which I gave the facetious answer, "So at last I'll know what the hell Jan Murray is talking about." Since that's an inside joke it naturally must be explained. Jan, a dear fellow and a funny one, often tells English language stories that have a Yiddish punch line.

The reason I go into this much detail in introducing the following lyric is that as soon as my brain, my mental computer, began to incorporate bits of Yiddish data, they were immediately made accessible to the other part of my brain that literally every day of my life conceives funny thoughts, jokes, ideas for monologues, light verse, comic sketches, or whatever. As I've mentioned earlier it's really not possible to adequately evaluate any song lyric if one knows nothing about its musical setting, but there's nothing much that can be done about that. So here's the lyric, which began to occur to me one morning, just as I was waking, and was completed in about five minutes.

(Perhaps it should be explained that the word leber *is pronounced like the English labor, as in Labor Day.)*

VERSE:
We've got lots of holidays
But never enough
There's Bulbas and Challeh Days
But sometimes it's tough
To get enough time off, from the daily grind
So hear my proposition, if you'll be so kind

CHORUS:
I take a day off;
I cool it awhile.
It's like a lay-off;
I'm startin' to smile,
'Cause it's Gehockta Leber Day,
Yeah, Gehockta Leber Day.

My brother, he works
Like all of the jerks
But mister, not me;
I'm perfectly free,
'Cause it's Gehockta Leber Day,
Yeah, Gehockta Leber Day.

You might not agree
But man, as for me
I'm free as the breeze;
I'm takin' my ease.
The park and the river,
They aren't chopped liver
So why don't the nation
Go take a vacation?
And as for the goyim,
Why should it annoy 'em?

When meshuga walks down the street
All the little birdies go tweet-tweet-tweet,
Tell Eberhard Faber to pencil it in
A brand new holiday
Makes me grin–

Hey, Doctuh
May sound fracockta
But it's Gehockta Leber–Day!

I'm Too Depressed to Sing the Blues

It occurred to me recently — oddly enough, for the first time in my long life — that there is something psychologically questionable about the social/cultural process known as "singing the blues." "The blues" is itself a phrase of interesting derivation. It is a shortened version of "the blue devils," first encountered in street slang sometime around 1850, which referred to that extreme form of alcoholic suffering, delirium tremens, a condition in which the alcohol addict suffers from frightening hallucinations, imagining he sees blue devils, pink elephants, or any other fantasy growing out of the fevered imagination.

After a few decades the reference to devils was dropped but the phrase still indicated a form of depression resulting from alcoholic excess and then — eventually — to depression generally. It was inevitable that the term would be brought into the popular lyric stream in which case its definition was even further narrowed so that it seemed to be related almost exclusively to misfortunes suffered in the context of love relationships.

But, to return to my original point, given that when we are depressed we are hardly likely to feel like singing I should have had this insight years earlier because there is often a playful element to blues lyrics and the singing performances of blues songs. St. Louis blues, for example, certainly does not indicate any either real or dramatically imagined state of depression on the part of the singer. In any event it was in speculating along these lines that the following comic lyric was written.

Now I'm so depressed tonight,
I'm too depressed to sing the blues
I mean when things ain't goin' right
Don't make no sense to sing the blues,
Now you know that's been true
Since the days of Charles Evans Hughes.

Cause, when you're really feelin' bad
Last thing you want to do is sing.
Yeah, when you're really feelin' sad,
Singin' is the dumbest thing.
Don't need no analytic session

To tell you that depression
Just makes you want to cry.
Don't need no really high IQ,
If your baby don't like you
All you want to do is lay right down and die.

So let me tell ya, friends and neighbors
You'll swear by all be-jabbers,
Don't need the 6 o'clock news
That when you're really feelin' rotten
Last thing you're gonna cotton to's
    the blues.

You know there ain't a single thing
That's gonna make you want to sing
So cut your squawkin', grab your walkin'
    shoes.
Just had to get it off my chest;
I'm too depressed
To sing the blues.

In a Little Dumb Cafe

(***A satire on French ballads of a certain type***)

There has always been a market, albeit a limited one, for funny songs. Some performers, such as Tom Leher and Allan Sherman, have worked only with such material. Numbers of this sort were much more common in the days of Vaudeville and in certain cases the success of a particular funny song became closely identified with the fate of the performer, as in the case of black comedian Bert Williams' delightful "Nobody."

"In a Little Dumb Cafe" is a satire on a particular kind of cabaret number more associated with European than American entertainment and more with Italy than France, England or Sweden. It should be performed with a pseudo-seriousness in which the mood of romantic drama is heightened for comic effect.

In a little dumb cafe
That's where I found you.
There were losers all around you
That rainy day.

You borrowed my umbrella
And gave it to another fella
But he was big and I was yella,
So what the hey?

In a little dumb cafe
Where the prices were outrageous
And young kids lied about their ages
Just to get a drink.

You were sitting at the bar
And I could tell
You'd gone too far
By the way you fell.

I knew 'twas time to walk away
From that little dumb cafe.

When I'm in Love

This song, which is from the score of the Broadway musical Sophie, *so far as I am aware addresses a theme not previously dealt with in the popular lyric field. Oddly enough I had dwelt on the subject matter many years earlier in a poem titled "Love Quickens All the Senses." It does seem that the elation characteristic of involvement in a romantic love relationship brings both the physical and psychological self to a feeling of well-being in which not only the beloved is appreciated but the beauties of nature as well.*

In this lyric I employ a device which is effective when properly placed, that of rhyming a word with one of the syllables of a subsequent word. In other words, instead of rhyming, say, resident *and* president, *in this case I rhymed* says *with the first syllable in the word* president.

I seem to need less sleep when I'm in love,
And still I don't count sheep when I'm in love,
And I need much less food when I'm in love,
And I am much less rude when I'm in love.
And every morning glory that I see
Seems to envy me.
You're rearranging me,
People see the change in me.
Everybody says—
I could run for president.

You make my heart just jump for joy;
You make this great big world a Christmas toy.
And there's a great big grin upon my face,
For the whole ever-lovin' human race.

I've got a few tricks I could teach the sun
In the blue above.
The reason I'm so lyrical,
Life is a miracle
When I'm in love.

If I Should Get to Heaven

There was a warm emotional sweetness to many of the popular songs of the early decades of this century and since I grew up in the 1920s and '30s I was, most fortunately, exposed to a good many such sentimental and romantic melodies and lyrics. The pleasure I derived from such superior material no doubt largely explains why, of the thousands of songs I have written over the years, romantic ballads have been the dominant form.

Whether there is, in fact, a heaven — indeed whether there is an afterlife of any sort — has been debated by philosophers down through the ages. But whether we are referring to fact or myth, popular thinking itself, in all times and places, is invariably heavily colored by background myths, legends and beliefs. It is highly unlikely that I'm the first person to wonder how most of us would feel — assuming that some form of heaven exists — if when we got there we realized that some of those we had most dearly loved were not present. In any event such a casual theological question gave rise to the following lyric.

If I should get to heaven
And found you weren't there,
Well, that could not be heaven,
That would not be fair
If I looked all around, dear,
And couldn't see your face
I'd search for you through endless time and space.

When time on earth is finished
If I found paradise,
Well, it would be diminished,
Quite a sad surprise
If I should get to heaven believing tales were true
And found myself alone–what would I do?

Here below,
One thing I know;
There is nothing sweeter than your love,
So I pray
That come that happy day
We'll go on forever up above.

If there is golden glory
Where angels sing and play
Well, I'll believe the story
If you're there that day.
If I should get to Heaven
And found there was no you
I'd think the ancient stories were untrue.

That Old Time Jazz

As I, and numerous others, have earlier observed, jazz is the only art form ever created in America. If too many of today's young people don't accord it appropriate respect perhaps they will be encouraged to do so by at least the knowledge that rock grew out of jazz in the 1920s, '30s and '40s. The leading jazz performers weren't noted only in their professional field, they were true national celebrities, and deservedly so, given that what they do is quite a remarkable accomplishment. Think of it — a jazz musician can play the same song a hundred times and perform it with fresh variations in each instance and, moreover, do so spontaneously.

The following lyric is simply a celebration of many of the jazz greats who have provided me such pleasure and inspiration during of my life.

I love all the stories they've told
About that old-time jazz.
How could anybody be cold
To all that old-time jazz?

Doncha love it when Satchmo plays
Some beautiful phrase
That makes the angels sing?

Rhythm and blues,
Whatever you choose.
The happy laughter
Makes the rafters ring.

Those hot licks
From Benny and Bix,
They made the whole world smile.

We had it made
When Ellington played
In that *Sophisticated Lady* style.

Folks, that was a wonderful age
With Cootie, and Roy
And "Hot Lips" Page.
Yeah, that was all pure gold

That wonderful old-
Time jazz.

It was really bold;
It rocked and it rolled.
I mean that old-time jazz.

First time you heard it
You were sold
On that wonderful old-time jazz.

Doncha dig it when Father Hines
Lays down those lines
The way he used to do?

You can either dance
Or sweet romance,
But you can never be blue.

No man says
He was better than Prez
At makin' your tootsies move.

And the Crosby band
For Dixieland
They really got ya in the groove.

Man, what swing!
What a wonderful thing
When Benny and Gene played *Sing, Sing, Sing*.

It was all pure gold
That wonderful old-
Time jazz!

There'll Come a Happy Day

The next number, which I wrote for an album recorded some years ago by a young folk singer named Linda Guymon, is an exercise in the Negro spiritual form.

There'll come a happy day, yes Lord, a happy day,
Waitin' for the sun to shine.
There'll come a better day, some red-letter day
For me and mine.

There'll come a sweeter day, full and completer day,
Ev'rybody's gonna sing
so keep the faith, my darlin',
And see what tomorrow will bring.

There'll come a lovely day, heavens-abovely day;
Won't that be fine?
There'll come a happy day, yes, Lord, a happy day,
Sooner than you all may think,
In the middle of this old desert,
We're gonna find cool water to drink.
Hallelujah! It's mighty long overdue,
But there's gonna be the happiest day
for me and you.

Index of Song Titles